A Modest Proposal: For Preventing Space Operations from Being a Burden to the Navy, and for Making the Space Cadre Beneficial to the Community

Paul V. Bandini and Andrew R. Dittmer

Nimble Books LLC: The AI Lab for Book-Lovers
~ Fred Zimmerman, Editor~

Humans and AI making books richer, more diverse, and more surprising.

Publishing Information

(c) 2023 Nimble Books LLC
ISBN: 978-1-60888-264-9

AI-generated Keyword Phrases

Navy space resources;
United States space systems;
Navy involvement in space;
Navy presence in space;
U.S. Space Force;
Navy space program;
Navy space organizations;
Navy space programs;
Navy space concepts;
Roles and responsibilities in Navy space;
Department of Defense space systems;
Navy Space Cadre;
Effective management of Navy space;
Operation of satellite systems;

COVER ART

The AI-generated prompt was:

Create a black and white illustration that captures the mood of this thesis, conveying a sense of ambition, innovation, and focus. The drawing should depict a dynamic scene set in space, with a commanding presence of a Navy ship soaring through the starry background. Show the ship surrounded by satellite systems, symbolizing the Navy's strong and expanding presence in space. The illustration should also portray a sense of collaboration and coordination, showing various entities within the Navy and Department of Defense working together seamlessly. Be sure to capture the determination and clarity of purpose that the thesis emphasizes, highlighting the Navy Space Cadre as key figures driving progress and setting clear goals. The author wants the reader to envision a future where satellite control and operations are streamlined and efficient, so elements like arrows or lines connecting the different satellites and organizations could be incorporated. Ultimately, the illustration should evoke a feeling of excitement and anticipation for a new era of navy advancements in space technology.

Publisher's Note

This 2007 thesis at the Naval Postgraduate School provides an instructive review of the reasons the US Navy has historically taken second place to the US Air Force in providing and utilizing military access to space, then puts forward proposals for improving the situation, notably, the formation of an independent Space Corps. Nearly twenty years later, the context has shifted, with the Navy ever more dependent on satellite services, and space-based surveillance a key element in the new "kill chain" of anti-ship ballistic and hypersonic weapons. The Navy, whose mission uniquely involves slow-moving persistence of large, not especially stealthy, objects over the vast expanses of the world's oceans, is also uniquely sensitive to the adversary capabilities afforded by small, extremely-fast-moving objects passing far overhead. Future naval wars with peer competitors will be inextricably connected with US military space capabilities.

Fred Zimmerman
Ann Arbor, Michigan, USA

FRONT MATTER

Publishing Information	ii
AI-generated Keyword Phrases	ii
Cover Art	iii
Abstracts	vi
TL;DR (one word)	vi
Explain It To Me Like I'm Five Years Old	vi
TL;DR (vanilla)	vi
Scientific Style	vi
Action Items	vii
Viewpoints	viii
Grounds for Dissent	viii
Red Team Critique	ix
MAGA Perspective	x
Page-by-Page Summaries	xii
Notable Passages	xxiii

Abstracts

TL;DR (One Word)

Streamlining.[1]

Explain It To Me Like I'm Five Years Old

This document is like a big report that talks about how the Navy uses space resources. It tells the history of space systems in the United States and how the Navy is involved. It says that the Navy should have a stronger presence in space and maybe even have its own space force. It talks about different groups and ideas related to the Navy's space program. It also talks about the different jobs and responsibilities of the Navy and the Department of Defense in space systems and communications.

TL;DR (Vanilla)

This thesis written in 2007 proposed a new approach to organizing and utilizing Navy space resources, emphasizing the need for a stronger Navy presence in space. It discusses the history of space systems in the United States and the Navy's involvement, as well as various organizations and programs related to the Navy's space program. The document highlights the importance of clear goals and objectives for effective management of the Navy Space Cadre. It also suggests consolidating satellite control functions under one organization for improved efficiency.

Scientific Style

This 2007 thesis explored the potential for a stronger Navy presence in space and the establishment of a U.S. Space Force. It examines the history and development of space systems in the United States, with an emphasis on the Navy's involvement. The document discusses various organizations,

---

[1] An interestingly apropos choice of words for a Service whose mission is moving giant streamlined objects through the oceans. — Ed.

programs, and concepts related to the Navy's space program, as well as the roles and responsibilities of entities within the Navy and the Department of Defense in relation to space systems and communications. It highlights the importance of the Navy Space Cadre and the need for clear goals and objectives for their effective management and operation. The document also addresses the challenges and issues surrounding the control and operation of satellite systems within the Department of Defense and proposes consolidating these functions under one organization for improved efficiency. The thesis advocates for a more streamlined and centralized approach to satellite control and operations.

ACTION ITEMS

Conduct a comprehensive review of the Navy's current space resources and capabilities.

Assess the potential benefits and drawbacks of establishing a U.S. Space Force within the Navy.

Develop clear goals and objectives for the Navy Space Cadre and establish a framework for their management and operation.

Explore options for consolidating satellite control and operations functions within the Department of Defense.

Identify potential areas for collaboration and partnership with other military branches and government agencies in the utilization of space resources.

Conduct a cost-benefit analysis of investing in new space systems and technologies for the Navy.

Develop a roadmap [or, if you will, plot a course.—Ed.]

VIEWPOINTS

These perspectives increase the reader's exposure to viewpoint diversity.

GROUNDS FOR DISSENT

A member of the organization responsible for this document might have had principled, substantive reasons to dissent from this report for several reasons.

Budgetary Concerns: One of the main reasons for dissent could be related to the potential cost implications of establishing a stronger Navy presence in space and creating a U.S. Space Force. The dissenting member might argue that the proposed changes would require significant financial commitments and divert resources from other critical areas within the Navy or Department of Defense.

Lack of Strategic Focus: The dissenting member may believe that the document fails to adequately address the strategic priorities and threats facing the United States in space. They may argue that the proposed construct does not align with the broader national security objectives or adequately consider potential adversaries' capabilities and intentions.

Redundancy and Overlapping Responsibilities: The dissenting member might contend that the proposed consolidation of satellite control and operations under one organization could create redundancy and overlapping responsibilities. They may argue that the current structure, with multiple organizations and programs, allows for greater flexibility and specialization in addressing various operational requirements and challenges.

Lack of International Cooperation: The document may fail to address the importance of international cooperation and partnerships in space exploration and utilization. The dissenting member might argue that a more collaborative approach, involving allied nations and organizations, would be more effective in achieving common goals and reducing duplication of efforts.

Potential Mission Creep: The dissenting member may raise concerns about the potential mission creep associated with establishing a U.S. Space Force. They may argue that expanding the Navy's role in space could lead to a militarization of outer space, triggering an arms race and undermining international treaties and agreements governing space activities.

Operational Challenges: The dissenting member might highlight operational challenges associated with the proposed construct. They may argue that consolidating satellite control and operations under one organization could lead to bureaucratic inefficiencies, slower decision-making processes, and a lack of agility in responding to emerging threats or technological advancements.

Lack of Public Support: The dissenting member may consider the lack of public support for a stronger Navy presence in space and the creation of a U.S. Space Force. They may argue that such initiatives could be seen as unnecessary militarization of space and a misallocation of resources, resulting in public backlash and potential negative consequences for the organization's reputation.

Overall, these principled, substantive reasons for dissent demonstrate the complexity and diverse perspectives within the organization responsible for the document. It highlights the need for careful consideration and analysis of alternative viewpoints to ensure the formulation of well-rounded and effective strategies.

RED TEAM CRITIQUE

Overall, the document provides a comprehensive overview of the history and development of space systems in the United States, focusing on the Navy's involvement. It effectively highlights the need for a stronger Navy presence in space and suggests the establishment of a U.S. Space Force to address this issue. The information provided on various organizations, programs, and concepts related to the Navy's space program is thorough and well-researched.

However, there are certain areas where the document could benefit from further improvement. Firstly, while it discusses the roles and responsibilities of entities within the Navy and the Department of Defense related to space systems and communications, it lacks a clear analysis of the current strengths and weaknesses of these entities. This analysis would provide a more accurate assessment of the need for a stronger Navy presence in space and the potential benefits of consolidating satellite control and operations.

Furthermore, the document could delve deeper into the challenges and issues surrounding the control and operation of satellite systems within the Department of Defense. It briefly mentions the need for improved efficiency but does not provide specific examples or proposed solutions. A more detailed analysis of these challenges and potential strategies for addressing them would strengthen the document's argument for a streamlined and centralized approach to satellite control and operations.

In terms of structure and organization, the document is generally cohesive and logical. However, it could benefit from better transitions between sections to create a smoother flow of ideas. Additionally, some sections could be expanded upon to provide more in-depth information and analysis.

Regarding writing style, the document is generally well-written, with clear and concise language. However, there are instances where technical jargon is used without sufficient explanation, which may make it difficult for non-technical readers to fully understand the content. Providing more context and definitions for specialized terms would enhance the document's accessibility and readability.

In conclusion, while the document provides a solid foundation for understanding the Navy's space program and the need for a more streamlined approach to satellite control and operations, there is room for improvement in terms of analysis, addressing challenges, and providing clearer explanations of technical terms. Taking these suggestions into consideration would strengthen the document's argument and make it more impactful.

MAGA Perspective

This document is just another example of the liberal agenda to expand government control and waste taxpayer dollars. The idea of a stronger Navy presence in space is nothing more than a ploy to further militarize our already bloated military-industrial complex. We should be focusing on fixing our problems here on Earth instead of wasting resources on a Space Force.

The mention of various organizations and programs related to the Navy's space program only shows how convoluted and bureaucratic our government has become. Instead of creating more layers of bureaucracy, we should be cutting unnecessary programs and reducing the size of government. This document fails to address these important issues.

The emphasis on the Navy Space Cadre and their goals and objectives is nothing more than bureaucratic jargon. We don't need more career politicians and bureaucrats telling us what to do. We need real leadership and a focus on American interests. This document misses the mark entirely.

The idea of consolidating satellite control under one organization may sound efficient on the surface, but it only serves to centralize power and control. We should be diversifying our satellite control capabilities and fostering competition. This document's suggestion is a step in the wrong direction.

Overall, this document is just another example of the liberal elite trying to push their globalist agenda. We need to stand up against this kind of thinking and focus on making America great again.

Page-by-Page Summaries[2]

2   *This page is a report on the need for the Navy to reorganize and prioritize its space resources, suggesting that the Navy should focus on leveraging space assets through the establishment of a capable Navy Space Cadre.*

4   *A proposal to prevent space operations from burdening the Navy and make the space cadre beneficial to the community.*

6   *The U.S. Navy needs to improve its integration of space capabilities and effects, and should consider relinquishing certain tasks to another service or agency. Instead, it should focus on developing a capable Navy Space Cadre to leverage space assets effectively.*

8   *This page provides a table of contents for a document that discusses the history of practical rocketry, developments during World War II, post-war cutbacks and competition, the Soviet threat, and the establishment of various military and space organizations.*

11   *The page lists space effects and space effects packages, provides a list of references, and an initial distribution list.*

14   *The page lists tables related to the Air Force's percentage of DoD space capabilities, NAVSOC functional control by location, and NAVSOC manning breakdown as of 2006.*

16   *This page provides a list of symbols, acronyms, and abbreviations related to the Air Force, space operations, and military command and control.*

18   *This page lists various acronyms related to geodetic satellite, global information grid, global positioning system, and other military and intelligence terms.*

19   *This page lists various abbreviations and acronyms related to military and space operations, including organizations such as NASA, NATO, and the National Security Space Institute.*

20   *This page provides a list of abbreviations and acronyms related to space operations in the Navy.*

21   *This page contains a list of acronyms related to military and communication terms.*

22   *This page provides a historical perspective on the development of U.S. space assets, with a focus on the Navy's involvement. It highlights the beginnings of practical rocketry and the influence of Dr. Robert Goddard's work.*

23   *Goddard's rocketry efforts were ridiculed in the US, but he found support from Daniel Guggenheim and formed the American Rocket Society. Lieutenant Fink Fischer offered Goddard a job with the US Navy, where he worked with Robert Truax on rocket-assisted takeoffs, known as JATO.*

24   *During World War II, Truax and Goddard developed the groundwork for the US Navy's guided missile program. They shifted their efforts to air-to-air and surface-to-air interceptor weapons. The German work during this time was well-funded and organized, resulting in the V-2 rocket. After the war, competition between the Army Air Corps and Navy space programs began.*

25   *Competition between military services and NASA led to specialization and struggles for control. Navy focused on space-based systems for terrestrial operations, while Army and Air Force focused on strategic dominance and force-enabling technologies. Inter-service*

---

[2] Page numbering in this and subsequent sections corresponds to the overprinted numbers applied to the original document, as **AI-1,** etc.

competition delayed joint development proposals. RAND report influenced the roles and responsibilities of the services.

26 *In the late 1940s and early 1950s, there were budget cuts and inter-service rivalries in the military. The Navy proposed a joint project with the Air Force for developing satellites, but it was rejected. Efforts in space-related activities were limited to studies. The Air Force was establishing its mission and facing reduced budgets.*

27 *The page discusses the establishment of satellite and space systems as an extension of strategic air power under the Air Force. It also mentions the development of the first U.S. satellite, Orbiter, and the competition between the Army's Vanguard and the Air Force's Project World Series.*

28 *The Vanguard program, chosen by the Navy for its perceived scientific nature, faced challenges due to its technological leap and lack of launch facilities. The Soviet launch of Sputnik led to negative public reaction towards Vanguard, prompting the establishment of ARPA and NASA.*

29 *The creation of ARPA and NASA disrupted the military's space efforts, leading to a centralization of funding and a loss of unique identity for individual service efforts.*

30 *The Vanguard program, faced with challenges and failures, led to increased government investment in space research. The Army and Air Force divided responsibilities for missile development, while the Navy focused on navigational systems and submarine-launched ballistic missiles.*

31 *The page discusses the development of ballistic missile forces by the Department of Defense to counter the Soviet threat. It highlights the joint Navy/Army program to develop the Fleet Ballistic Missile (Polaris) and the impact of this program on changing Navy practices. Additionally, it mentions the development of the Transit satellite navigation system by Johns Hopkins Applied Physics Laboratory.*

32 *The page discusses the development of the Transit system, the predecessor to the GPS system, and the establishment of the Air Force as the lead agency for military space systems development.*

33 *The 1961 Department of Defense Directive 5160.32 slowed down military space development, but the Army and Navy continued their own science and technology development. The Army developed the Defense Satellite Communication System (DSCS) and the Navy conducted various experiments and engineering developments in space-related fields.*

34 *The page discusses the development of the Navy's space program, including the successful use of gravity gradient stabilization techniques and the Transit navigation system. It also mentions the divergence between the Navy and Air Force in the 1970s, leading to problems with the FLTSAT program.*

35 *The page discusses the clash of organizational cultures in the military space arena and the establishment of the United States Space Command and growth of naval space efforts. It also mentions the leveraging of space systems and other service capabilities to reduce the Navy's investment in space.*

36 *The creation of the United States Space Command in 1985 was driven by the need for centralized control of military space efforts and the development of the Strategic Defense Initiative. The Army's doctrine of combat, AirLand Battle, heavily relied on space systems infrastructure.*

37 *The page discusses the establishment and functions of the Army Space Command and the Naval Space Command, which served as a central point for various Navy space-related organizations.*

38	*Naval Space Command's importance grew in the 1990s, with responsibilities including UHF communications and monitoring missile launches. However, the Air Force and Intelligence Community resisted Navy's involvement in space operations, reflecting a historical proprietary attitude towards space.*
39	*The Air Force aims to exert control over the air and space environments, as seen in a 1961 article. However, the use of the term "Aerospace" has been questioned since the 1990s, as it dilutes the focus on air superiority.*
40	*Navy space efforts have declined due to increased Air Force budgets, restrictions on service exploitation of space, and lack of leadership recognition. The decline may also be attributed to the reorganization of Department of Defense space management during the Clinton Administration.*
41	*The page discusses the organizational changes and restructuring of the Department of Defense's space programs and architecture from 1995 to 2003, resulting in disinterest from senior Navy leadership.*
42	*The Navy's incorporation of the Naval Space Command into NETWARCOM resulted in a loss of direction for the Navy space community. The Air Force had a significantly larger share of the Department of Defense space budget and capabilities. The Navy has relied on other organizations for its combat requirements, but has faced quality-of-service concerns with these resources.*
43	*Incompatible mindsets between space operators and users led to dissatisfaction, but restructuring improved operational space support. The Navy's interest in space has diminished, relying on outsourcing and other organizations for space-based capabilities. This reflects a larger struggle as the Navy defines its role in asymmetric warfare.*
44	*The Navy's focus on space systems development and operation needs to be sharpened and refined, separating unnecessary services and functions from those that best support the institution's goals and warfighting responsibilities.*
46	*This page provides an overview of the organizations and concepts related to the United States Navy's space program, including the establishment of the 2001 Space Commission to assess national security space management and organizations.*
47	*The page discusses the importance of space as a national security priority and the role of Naval Network Warfare Command in leveraging space capabilities for the Navy.*
48	*The page discusses the NETWARCOM Maritime Operations Center (MOC) Space Cell, which provides space situational awareness and support to fleet forces. It also mentions the Naval Satellite Operations Center (NAVSOC), responsible for operating and maintaining satellite systems for the Navy.*
49	*NAVSOC controls satellites from five remote ground stations in the US and Guam. Table 2 lists the functions performed by NAVSOC for each satellite, including T&C, Doppler collection, and orbit determination.*
50	*NAVSOC is the controlling authority for the Mobile-User Objective System (MUOS) and plans to take control of the bus for five MUOS satellites by 2015. The concept of a Maritime Headquarters with Maritime Operations Center (MHQ with MOC) is being developed to better support operational-level planning, execution, and assessment. The Carrier Strike Group (CSG) is a flexible maritime combat-force organization centered on an aircraft carrier.*
51	*The page discusses the Joint Space Operations Center (JSpOC) and its role in planning, directing, and assessing space forces. It also mentions the Government Accountability Office (GAO) and its mission to support Congress in improving government performance and accountability.*

52	*SPAWAR provides information management technology for the Navy's missions. PEO Space Systems manages and procures narrowband communications satellites for the DoD.*
53	*The page discusses the role and responsibilities of the Program Executive Officer (PEO) Space Systems in the Navy, including their reporting structure and interface with other national security space organizations. It also mentions the mission of the Navy's Communications Satellite Program Office (PMW-146) to acquire space-based communications systems.*
54	*PMW-146 is the Navy's major buyer of communication satellites, continuing to meet warfighters' needs using innovative technology. The NRO designs and operates reconnaissance satellites for various government agencies. The NRL conducts scientific research and development for the Navy and Marine Corps.*
55	*The Navy Center for Space Technology develops and acquires space systems for naval missions, including spacecraft, ground control stations, and operational concepts. Sea Power 21 is the Navy's vision to transform and meet future challenges by aligning with other services and generating maximum combat power.*
56	*"Sea Power 21" is a strategy that aims to enhance maritime power through expanded power projection, global defensive assurance, and enhanced operational independence. ForceNet serves as the framework for naval warfare in the information age. Coordinating Authority is defined as a commander responsible for coordinating specific functions or activities involving multiple military departments or forces.*
57	*The page discusses the roles and responsibilities of the Space Authority and Space Coordinating Authority in joint space operations planning.*
58	*The Joint Warfighting Space concept aims to provide responsive space and near-space capabilities to support the joint force commander in military operations. It requires a dedicated and knowledgeable Navy space cadre to meet Navy needs and requirements.*
59	*Space effects and space effects packages are utilized in the Fleet through the Space Effects Package (SEP) to provide necessary products for mission success. The SEP process includes a Space Assessment and Space Operations Plan. Understanding Navy space efforts and terminology is crucial for redefining Navy space efforts.*
60	*The United States Navy has undergone a significant transformation in its space efforts from 2003 to 2007, focusing on delivering space capabilities to increase combat effectiveness. The evolution of the Naval Space Campaign is traced back to the 2001 Space Commission findings and current policies that designate the Air Force as the Department of Defense Executive Agent for Space. The establishment of a Navy Space Cadre was also approved during this time.*
61	*The page discusses the Department of the Navy Space Policy, emphasizing the importance of maintaining and utilizing space systems for tactical purposes. It highlights the need for a competent Navy Space Cadre and representation in joint and national space processes.*
62	*The page discusses the organizational structure and policies related to the Navy's space program, including the establishment of a Navy Space Cadre and the management of satellite communications resources.*
63	*The page discusses the Navy's Space Cadre Human Capital Strategy, which aims to groom and shape the workforce to fill decision-making positions in the space assessment, acquisition, and operational arena. It also mentions a CNO instruction that establishes procedures for implementing the Department of the Navy Space Policy.*

64	The page discusses the responsibilities of the Deputy CNO and Naval Network Warfare Command in managing the Navy Space Cadre and formulating space policy. It also mentions the Naval Space Campaign Plan and its role in improving space processes across the naval enterprise.
65	The Navy Space Campaign Plan focuses on developing space requirements, improving combat effectiveness, and cultivating expertise in the Navy Space Cadre. It does not mention the acquisition or management of narrow-band communications satellites.
66	The Navy is actively coordinating its space needs and capabilities with other branches and the civil space community. They are developing a new Navy Space Concept of Operations document and following the U.S. National Space Policy to ensure excellence in space activities. The Navy's space policy includes positive aspects such as the establishment of a Navy Space TYCOM and the Fleet Space Handbook. The designation of NETWARCOM as the Navy's Space Type Commander has potential for progress.
67	The Navy's space policies and plans lack clarity on the structure and operation of Navy-controlled satellites, as well as the usage and allocation of unclassified space assets. There is also a lack of consolidated command and control architecture for naval space operations.
68	Navy space policies lack guidance on establishing and maintaining a space cadre and joint space endeavors. The lack of direction hinders the success of the Navy Space Campaign and requires a critical revision of Naval Space policy. The Navy-wide space Command and Control structure is unclear and needs to be formally published.
69	This page provides a historical command relationship organization chart for the Naval Satellite Operations Center and discusses the importance of understanding how space effects are delivered to the warfighter.
70	CSG-8 used a structure to maximize space effects during their deployment, which will be incorporated into the new Navy Space CONOPS. The benefits of this construct were essential to CSG-8's operations and improved their use of space capabilities.
71	The page discusses the success of the Navy's space operations and outlines future plans for the Navy Space Campaign, including formalizing space training and incorporating space play into exercises.
72	The page discusses the shortcomings of the current Navy Space Campaign and emphasizes the need for a clear implementation strategy and leadership to navigate future challenges.
74	The Navy Space Cadre was established in response to a Department of Defense directive, and is parallel to the Air Force, Army, and Marine Corps Space Cadres. This chapter examines the formation and roles of the Navy's Space Cadre, comparing it to the other services' Space Cadres.
75	The page discusses the role of organization and management in national security space capabilities. It emphasizes the need for national leadership to prioritize space and suggests merging various space activities to improve accountability and effectiveness. It also highlights the importance of sustaining a cadre of skilled professionals in the field.
76	The page discusses the importance of investing in career development, education, and training for military and civilian space professionals. It also mentions the establishment of Space Cadres within the Department of Defense and the Navy's creation of a Navy Space Cadre.
77	The Navy's approach to organizing its Space Cadre has led to a lack of organizational momentum and deficiencies in Human Capital Strategy, according to a 2004 GAO

	report. The Navy lacks clear goals and objectives for its space cadres, unlike the Air Force and Marine Corps.
78	The Navy's approach to organizing and managing its space personnel has been ineffective, lacking clear leadership and certification procedures. Unlike other branches, the Navy does not have a designated community for space professionals, resulting in a lack of support and funding. The Air Force, on the other hand, has established policies and procedures for its space personnel.
79	The Air Force's space cadre lacks operational expertise and understanding of terrestrial warfighter needs, requiring remediation by experienced Army and Marine Corps members. The Army has a robust program for its space cadre, while the Air Force's perception of their own space "operators" and interpretation of the term differ.
80	The page discusses the 2004 GAO report on the DoD Space Human Capital Resources Strategy, highlighting implementation failings and the quick response of the Executive Agent for Space. It also mentions the seriousness with which the Air Force approaches space planning and policy.
81	The page discusses the development and implementation of education and training programs, certification processes, and management functions for space professionals in the military.
82	The Air Force and Marine Corps have different approaches to space systems. The Air Force sees space as a core competency and is responsible for all aspects of space-related endeavors. The Marine Corps has a smaller space cadre focused on providing representation and support for Marine Corps missions. The Navy, on the other hand, lacks clarity and direction in its Space Cadre efforts.
83	The page discusses the lack of effective space cadre management systems in the Navy and Army, with the Navy being the furthest behind. The Navy's space policy lacks specific metrics and goals, while the Army has made progress in identifying personnel and positions.
84	The Navy implemented a strategy to improve the use of its Space Human Capital, following criticism and recommendations. The strategy outlines specific missions, membership requirements, and leadership positions for the Navy Space Cadre. Centralization of organization and planning was prioritized.
85	Navy Space Cadre Advisor has been instrumental in improving the Navy's efforts in codifying requirements and responsibilities for the Navy Space Cadre. Fit and fill rates for Navy Space Cadre personnel have increased since the implementation of the Navy Space Human Capital Strategy.
86	The page shows historical fit and fill rates for the Space Systems Operations Subspecialty. It also highlights several issues that the Navy Space Cadre Human Capital Strategy does not address.
87	The page discusses various measures that need to be taken to improve the integration and career progression of enlisted space experts within the Navy Space Cadre. These measures have been identified as shortfalls in the Navy's strategy and have already been solved by other services such as the Air Force and Army.
88	The Navy Space Cadre faces problems due to leadership dysfunction and lack of understanding. The Navy should acknowledge and implement joint training, core competencies, career requirements, and common certifications like other services. Promotion boards have included language to promote and retain personnel with space education and experience.

89	*The page discusses the promotion rates for Navy Space Cadre members and the efforts to recognize their accomplishments through additional qualification designations and subspecialty codes.*
90	*The Navy's qualification system for space personnel is confusing and needs clarification. The qualification levels are VS1 (Recruit), VS2 (Apprentice), VS3 (Journeyman), and VS4 (Expert), but it is unclear if these codes accurately identify highly qualified individuals for promotion. The labeling system for AQDs and Subspecialty Codes adds to the confusion.*
91	*The Navy Space Cadre has a majority of ashore positions, which undermines its credibility with seagoing communities. The Navy is considering eliminating shore-based jobs to save costs, but this could result in unfilled needs for space systems. There is a need for officers in space billets to have operational experience at sea.*
92	*The page discusses the need for Space Cadre officers to have operational experience and expertise in space systems. It highlights the limited utilization of the degree provided by the Naval Postgraduate School and emphasizes the importance of practical experience and interaction with the greater DoD space community. It also mentions the challenges faced in providing commanders with desired information and services without adequate understanding and expertise.*
93	*The implementation of space-related duties in the Navy is hindered by the fact that they are considered secondary to primary job assignments. However, there have been exceptions, such as the robust space training and education given to Carrier Strike Group 8. The objectives of this training include developing maritime-specific space requirements and increasing fleet understanding of space-provided effects.*
94	*The page discusses the need to improve combat effectiveness and human capital in the Navy's use of space-based capabilities. It also emphasizes the importance of understanding space system vulnerabilities and implementing best practices through doctrine and policy. The success of a previous experiment is attributed to the efforts of an individual, highlighting the need for more widespread commitment and support.*
95	*The page discusses the need for a dedicated Space Operations officer on Strike Group Staffs and the growth of the Navy Space Cadre in numbers and influence.*
96	*The Navy Space Cadre has a mismatch between the number of personnel trained in space-related jobs and the number of available positions. Additionally, the Navy is underrepresented in military space efforts, with most positions located outside of the Navy organization.*
97	*The Navy should adopt methods and systems used by the Air Force to enhance jointness and reduce redundancies in planning and management of the Space Cadre. The Army's acceptance of Air Force training and certification is a good example of simplicity and synergy. Strategic integration of service efforts in maintaining and furthering their Space Cadres is a viable option. The Navy needs experts in space systems and operations to support its reliance on space systems. Highly trained personnel with substantial space expertise can promote the Navy Space Cadre and*
98	*The Navy's space operations and expertise are threatened by a lack of leadership understanding and neglect. This chapter examines the current state of the Navy's space systems, support to operational forces, and acquisition programs, and discusses alternatives for improvement.*
99	*The current Department of Defense structure for controlling communications satellites is convoluted and fragmented, with multiple agencies involved. Consolidating these functions under one organization would reduce costs and simplify operations.*

	Commercial sector satellite operations have already centralized and simplified management tasks through automation.
100	*The page discusses the role of the 50th Space Wing and 50th Space Communications Squadron in operating and maintaining over 170 Department of Defense satellites. It also mentions the mission areas of the Naval Satellite Operations Center.*
101	*The page discusses the different satellite operations missions of the Air Force, Navy, and Army, highlighting the complexity and overlap in control and responsibilities.*
102	*The page discusses the redundancies in the current satellite control structure and suggests that the Navy should transfer its satellite operation responsibilities to the Air Force's 50th Space Wing.*
103	*The United States Navy and Marine Corps must maintain their ability to use space systems and participate in the changing NSS environment. The Navy is fulfilling a role as a "ruthless customer" of space capabilities, regardless of who provides them. The Naval Satellite Operations Center's efforts are increasingly marginalized by the Air Force Space Command.*
104	*The page discusses the potential elimination of the Navy component of the satellite command and control function, as automation and mission reduction have reduced the need for personnel. The merger with the Air Force's 14th Air Force and 50th Space Wing is proposed, as existing facilities and command relationships support this change.*
105	*The page provides information on the facilities and locations of the NAVSOC organization, as well as the personnel breakdown. It suggests that the 50th Space Wing could take control of NAVSOC locations and personnel, with a focus on reassigning Navy personnel to joint or Air Force activities.*
106	*The page provides a snapshot of the daily operations at NAVSOC, showing the functions performed by the Naval Satellite Operations Center. The small quantity of systems and contact events managed by NAVSOC is significantly less compared to the Air Force Satellite Control Network.*
107	*The page discusses the operations of the Air Force Satellite Control Network (AFSCN) and the benefits of incorporating NAVSOC operations into 14th Air Force and 50th Space Wing. It questions the superiority of NAVSOC's service and system reliability compared to the Air Force.*
108	*The page discusses the advantages of incorporating Naval Satellite Operations into the Air Force's satellite control system, including centralizing responsibility, simplifying funding and administration, and eliminating redundancy. It also mentions the need for improved representation of service-specific needs and addresses the complaints of the satellite user community.*
109	*The NNWC MOC Space Cell is redundant and unnecessary as it serves as a middleman between the JSpOC and maritime users, adding an unnecessary layer to the space support hierarchy. The JSpOC already has the necessary expertise to support all users, including maritime forces.*
110	*The page discusses the elimination of the NNWC Space Cell and the need for increased Navy presence in the JSpOC for more efficient space resource assistance and information distribution.*
111	*The page discusses the Navy's involvement in space systems acquisition, including the establishment of the Program Executive Office (PEO) Space Systems and the Communications Satellite Program Office. The Navy coordinates with other organizations to ensure the purchase of appropriate space systems for national security goals.*

112   PMW-146 is responsible for acquiring and fielding UHF satellite systems for the Navy. It is currently focused on the Mobile User Objective System (MUOS) and is considered a successful acquisition program in the midst of failures. PMW-146 is part of the PEO Space Systems, which was established to centralize space system functions within the Navy.

113   The Navy no longer has a need for UHF satellite communications due to advancements in technology and the shift towards high-bandwidth systems. The Naval Studies Board suggests that the Navy should consider relieving itself of the MUOS program, as it is no longer a priority.

114   The Navy should divest its development and acquisition of satellite systems to the Air Force, allowing for better allocation of resources. The Navy's space-related budget is mainly allocated to satellite communications, and transferring control of communication satellites to the Air Force would likely result in a loss of funds for the Navy.

115   The page discusses the transfer of narrowband satellite communication programs from the Navy to the Air Force, which may result in cost savings and the strengthening of the Navy's space research and technology development efforts. The Naval Research Laboratory is highlighted as a key player in these endeavors.

116   The NRL is the lead Navy activity for space technology and systems development. It has a narrower focus on research and science and aligns with the Navy's traditional funding and customer paradigm.

117   The Naval Center for Space Technology focuses on advanced science and technology for the Navy and National Security Space community. It allows for more productive research, simplifies technology transfer, and enables partnering relationships with other organizations. The Naval Research Laboratory's expertise in space-based systems led to funding from various non-Navy organizations.

118   NRL's ability to develop and launch new satellite systems for the Navy has diminished due to lack of funding. Re-invigorating NRL and utilizing talent within the NRO and Navy is crucial for centralizing and simplifying space systems requirements and capabilities.

119   The page discusses the importance of improving human capital and cultural change within the Navy Space organization. It suggests utilizing Navy Space Cadre officers, researchers, and personnel from the Naval Research Laboratory to enhance communication, understanding, and requirements definition in space-related endeavors.

120   The Navy's space efforts have been decentralized and fragmented, hindering their ability to meet future needs. They should transfer their programmatic and acquisition efforts to another agency and focus on science and technology R&D and the promotion of a Navy Space Cadre.

122   The Navy should focus on science and technology research instead of operational control of communication satellites, establish a stronger Navy Space Cadre, and redefine its role in the acquisition process to maximize the effectiveness of future Navy space efforts.

123   The Navy's efforts in establishing a space cadre have been criticized, but progress has been made with the establishment of NETWARCOM and the trial run of a CSG Staff Space Officer. However, there is a need for more clarity in doctrine and leadership involvement in the joint space environment. The Navy Space Cadre is still facing challenges in utilization and detailing processes.

124   Advocacy is needed to gain recognition and resources for the Navy Space Cadre. The Navy should consider transferring control of space assets to the Air Force for better

	efficiency. Space power is crucial for military operations and provides significant advantages.
125	*The page discusses the need for further analysis and research on the Department of Defense's future efforts in space utilization for warfighting. It suggests establishing a separate career path for Navy Space Officers, highlighting potential benefits and drawbacks.*
126	*The page discusses the potential creation of a U.S. Space Force and the need for a separate space force to maximize the use of space in military operations. It suggests that a Navy perspective on the subject would be valuable.*
127	*The Navy's leadership lacks understanding of the complexities of space operations and there is a need for clearer policies and guidance. Efforts to improve Navy space endeavors are underway but further refinement is needed for organizational success in space programs.*
128	*Investment in space and science will ensure a bright future for the organization.*
130	*This appendix provides further detail on the definitions mentioned in Chapter II, including the establishment and members of the U.S. Commission to Assess National Security Space Management and Organizations (2001 Space Commission).*
131	*The page discusses recommendations from a commission on national security space management and organization, including the establishment of space as a priority, the appointment of a Presidential Space Advisory Board, and the assignment of responsibilities within the Department of Defense.*
132	*NETWARCOM is designated as the lead for the Naval Space Campaign and oversees the Navy space cadre. NAVSOC operates satellite constellations for communication and research purposes. The NIOSC Space Cell provides support and coordination for maritime space requirements at both the operational and tactical levels.*
134	*The page discusses the Naval Satellite Operations Center (NAVSOC) and the Maritime Headquarters with Maritime Operations Center (MHQ-MOC), highlighting their roles in military operations.*
135	*The page provides information about the composition and roles of a typical Carrier Strike Group, which includes a carrier, cruiser, destroyers, submarine, and supply ship. The group can be employed for various purposes such as protecting shipping, supporting amphibious forces, and establishing naval presence.*
136	*The Joint Space Operations Center (JSpOC) develops global and theater space operations strategies, produces task orders, and conducts assessments. The Government Accountability Office (GAO) issues reports and testimony to Congress, operating under strict professional standards of review.*
137	*SPAWAR is the Navy's C4ISR command for acquiring and managing communication and warfare systems. PEO Space Systems is responsible for space-related programs.*
138	*The page provides information about the Navy Communications Satellite Program Office (PMW-146) and the National Reconnaissance Office (NRO), which plays a primary role in achieving information superiority for the US Government and Armed Forces.*
139	*The page discusses the National Reconnaissance Office and the Naval Research Laboratories, including their missions and responsibilities in relation to U.S. national security.*
140	*The Naval Center for Space Technology is the lead Navy activity for space technology development and mapping. It focuses on developing space systems to meet mission requirements with improved performance and efficiency. The Spacecraft Engineering*

	Department serves as the focal point for the Navy's spacecraft bus capability and provides analysis, design, and hardware expertise in various areas.
141	*SEA POWER 21 is a strategic plan for the Navy that focuses on three concepts: SEA SHIELD, SEA STRIKE, and the SEA BASE. It also includes initiatives for developing sailors, testing new concepts and technologies, and capturing efficiencies. FORCEnet is the overarching effort to integrate various elements of naval operations.*
142	*The page discusses the Navy's plan to implement network-centric warfare through FORCEnet. It also mentions coordinating authority and its role in coordinating specific functions and activities involving different military departments or forces.*
143	*The page discusses the roles and responsibilities of coordinating authorities in interagency activities, specifically focusing on space operations and planning. It highlights the importance of coordination, integration, and prioritization of space capabilities for joint force objectives.*
144	*The page discusses the responsiveness and integration of space capabilities, as well as the assessment and plan for space effects and vulnerabilities.*
145	*The page discusses force enhancement techniques, including the use of overhead non-imaging infrared technology to detect infrared activity near the Strike Group, as well as the tasks of MASINT and IMINT in supporting the ISR Plan.*
146	*A list of references on various topics related to military and space capabilities, including network-centric warfare, theater coordination of global space capabilities, the Rumsfeld Space Commission, and United States national security space management and organization.*
150	*This page contains a list of various sources and references related to space and maritime partnerships in the military.*
151	*This page contains a list of various sources related to the military's use of space, including reports, interviews, and white papers.*
154	*The page contains a list of individuals and organizations that have received an initial distribution of a document or report.*

NOTABLE PASSAGES

6 *"Lack of clear direction in analysis and identification of current and future requirements for space-related capabilities presents a hazard to implementation of the tenants of Sea Power 21 and Navy participation in future conflicts."*

22 *"Apropos of the gradual collapse of the Roman Empire, the house of Navy Space has slid into disrepair from its heights in the 1940s and 1980s."*

23 *"The negative press had the effect of damaging Goddard's credibility with the mainstream American scientific and military establishment, and despite repeated offers of service to the government, he was turned down multiple times in the years before World War II."*

24 *"Truax identifies this study as the first U.S. space program – the document proposed the construction, launch and operation of an earth-orbiting satellite for scientific purposes."*

25 *"To its credit, this particular RAND document, 'Preliminary Design of an Experimental World-Circling Spaceship' proved to be a seminal document, offering predictions regarding the importance of scientific instruments on orbital spacecraft and the public impact of national efforts to put men in space. Additionally, the RAND report provided ammunition to the Air Staff of the Army that '...Army Air Forces should have primary responsibility for any military satellite vehicle, considering such activity to be essentially an extension of strategic air power.' This statement set the stage for the next sixty years worth of competition between the Navy and the Air Force in the arena of strategic force application and the roles and responsibilities of the services."*

26 *"In 1948, the Secretary of Defense reported, with respect to space: The Committee on guided Missiles recommended that efforts in the field (of earth satellite vehicles) be limited to studies."*

28 *"Validating the RAND report 'Preliminary Design of and Experimental World-Circling Spaceship' negative American public reaction to the Soviet success was directed against the Vanguard project, which because of the array of unproven technologies involved, was well behind the Soviet schedule."*

29 *"With the founding of NASA and ARPA, the age of independent military service development of space systems came to an end. The centralization of funding under ARPA, the nascent bureaucracy of NASA, and the transfer of so much institutional expertise from the military services to NASA resulted in a watering-down of the culture that identified the individual military service efforts as unique."*

30 *"Following the two-year spasm of effort that comprised the Vanguard program, government investment and research in space scaled up dramatically. As the money began to flow in, the individual services were able to diversify and de-conflict their efforts in utilizing the capabilities enabled by space development."*

31 *"The joint program leveraged the Army's experience in booster development, and levied the requirement on the Navy to develop the sea-based launching system. Initially beneficial for both the Army and Navy, the program provided the Army with a*

	requirement to defend against Air Force encroachment, and the Navy a method to get into the strategic weapons business."
32	"By 1961, the modern scheme of military satellite launch and operation had begun to emerge. Secretary of Defense Robert McNamara signed Defense Directive 5160.32 in March of 1961, assigning the Air Force sole responsibility for development and acquisition of all U.S. military space systems. The other services were permitted to perform research in space systems and technology, but were not allowed to field in-house developed systems. Driven by a January 1961 report headed up by Dr. Jerome Wiesner of MIT (later, President Emeritus of MIT) that attributed the Soviet lead in space to lack of coordination and duplicated efforts by the U.S. military establishment, the Secretary of the Air Force lobbied the Office of the
35	"Growing reliance on space as a medium to support terrestrial naval operations began to meet with high-level recognition in the Navy in the early 1980s, and in 1983, the Secretary of the Navy stood up Naval Space Command to centralize control of naval space efforts."
36	"U.S. Space Command came into existence in-part because of the institutional inertia developed during the early 1980s to centralize control of military space efforts, and also because of the extensive R&D being conducted for the Strategic Defense Initiative, President Ronald Reagan's space-based weapons system for anti-ballistic weapons defense."
38	"As U.S. national space capabilities matured towards the end of the 20th century, the organizations that developed the greatest capability, acquired the largest budgets and established the most lengthy personnel rosters began to approach space as if it were their exclusive provenance. This proprietary attitude hearkens back to the 1961 DoD Directive naming the Air Force as the Executive Agent for Space and the 1960 founding of the National Reconnaissance Office (NRO). Notwithstanding the cancellation of this directive in 1970, as space budgets and programs migrated to these two organizations beginning in the 1960s, they forged an institutional mentality that much as the Navy 'ownership' of the seas was uncontested by the other services, the Air…"
39	"No existing programs were changed. The Army will continue with its Advent communications satellite; the Navy will stick with its Transit navigation satellite. And each service, in Pentagon parlance, will have 'the right to think,' to do research on the problems of putting its weapons into space. But from now on, the Air Force is boss of the big boosters that make military space ventures possible."
40	"In the face of increasing Air Force space budgets, restrictions on service exploitation of the space arena and ambivalence from leadership, Navy space efforts are under-represented in comparison with the relative importance of space effects and space support to the fleet. The mid-1990s represented the pinnacle of the modern Navy space organization. During these years, in the aftermath of Desert Storm, leadership and 'warfighter' recognition of the Navy's reliance on robust satellite systems for command, control, communications and intelligence (C^3I) functions reached its peak."
41	"The result of this gusty and shifting organizational climate seems to have resulted in disinterest and indifference on the part of senior Navy leadership."
42	"Unfortunately, quality-of-service concerns in many facets of the National Security Space mission areas, relating to both USAF- and Intelligence Community-provided resources have plagued this relationship."
43	"Fortunately, restructuring initiatives in the late 1990s, resulting from DoD and congressional concerns about space support to military forces during the 1991 Gulf War, relieved some of the friction. Although elements of this problem persist, operational space

	support of the terrestrial warfighter has improved dramatically since this restructuring of management of National Security Space functions in the late 1990s."
44	*"In an environment of meager budgets, minimal manpower and apparent leadership disinterest, modern-day maintenance of space capabilities has primarily been the result of dedicated individuals and isolated pockets of corporate expertise."*
45	*n/a*
46	*"Senator Bob Smith (R-N.H.) was the point person in Congress for the creation of the Space Commission. Smith believed that the annual defense budgets were continually short-changing space programs. He also noticed that military personnel without space backgrounds were being promoted faster than those with space experience and he alleged that treaties had negotiated away the U.S. advantages in space."*
47	*"The commission determined that the United States should take immediate steps to develop superior space capabilities."*
50	*"The concept of a Maritime Headquarters with Maritime Operations Center (MHQ with MOC) evolved from Flag-level deliberations concerning the roles and capabilities of the US Navy at the operational-level of war (OLW). There is a breach between the current tactical expertise of the US Navy and enduring CCDR requirements to support theater-wide strategies and national objectives. The Navy must modify command organizations in Echelons II and III (NCCs, Numbered Fleet commanders and principal headquarters commanders) to better support operational-level planning, execution and assessment. The establishment of MHQs with MOC will support execution of the National Strategy on Maritime Security (NSMS), comply with CNO 2006 Guidance, and fulfill CCDR requirements specified in the Unified Command*
51	*"The Government Accountability Office, the audit, evaluation and investigative arm of Congress, exists to support Congress in meeting its constitutional responsibilities and to help improve the performance and accountability of the federal government for the American people."*
53	*"The Program Executive Officer also provides a unique interface to other national security space organizations through his concurrent assignments as Commander, SPAWAR Space Field Activity (SSFA) and as Director, Communications Directorate, National reconnaissance Office (NRO), enabling a continuing partnership and effective integration of space systems expertise and best practices across the Navy-DoD-Intelligence Community interface."*
55	*"Sea Power 21" is the Navy's vision to align, organize, integrate, and transform to meet the challenges that lie ahead. It requires us to continually and aggressively reach. It is global in scope, fully joint in execution, and dedicated to transformation. It reinforces and expands concepts being pursued by the other services—long-range strike; global intelligence, surveillance, and reconnaissance; expeditionary maneuver warfare; and light, agile ground forces—to generate maximum combat power from the joint team.*
56	*"Sea Power 21" will employ current capabilities in new ways, introduce innovative capabilities as quickly as possible, and achieve unprecedented maritime power. Decisive warfighting capabilities from the sea will be built around: Sea Strike—expanded power projection that employs networked sensors, combat systems, and warriors to amplify the offensive impact of sea-based forces; Sea Shield—global defensive assurance produced by extended homeland defense, sustained access to littorals, and the projection of defensive power deep overland; Sea Basing—enhanced operational independence and support for joint forces provided by networked, mobile, and secure sovereign platforms operating in the maritime domain. ForceNet is the "glue" that binds together Sea Strike, Sea Shield, and Sea Basing*

58 "The JWS concept features the delivery of responsive space and near-space capabilities to directly support the joint force commander in a theater across the range of military operations, with emphasis at the operational and tactical warfighting levels. It is envisioned as a rapid reaction, networked set of space and near-space capabilities dedicated to the JFC and integrated with National Security Space and organic theater systems."

59 "Knowledge gained from exposure to the definitions and concepts that encompass the United States Navy space efforts provides a functional baseline of understanding for future arguments contained in follow-on chapters within this thesis. Comprehension and recognition of space terminology and conceptual ideology are necessary to appreciate the full effect of these arguments. In addition, exposure to the numerous and sometimes confusing Navy space policy documents and instructions is also necessary to ensure desired effects are achieved when pondering the proposed argument of redefining Navy space efforts."

60 "The Naval Space Campaign is operational and aggressive, focused on delivering space capabilities to the warfighter to increase combat effectiveness."

61 "The United States Navy and Marine Corps must maintain their ability to tactically exploit the capabilities provided by space systems and participate in all appropriate aspects of the changed NSS environment in order to function as an integrated member of the Nation's joint warfighting team...the DoN must continually reassess its approach and investment to ensure that naval forces receive the maximum benefit of space-based capabilities."

62 "Successful application of space in the Navy translates to a healthy and robust Navy Space Cadre."

63 "Proper management and placement of Navy Space Cadre personnel will allow the Navy to gain huge return on investment and leverage more than $12B per year spent on unclassified space systems by the Air Force and other services."

64 "The wording of this instruction suggests a number of interpretations. One suggestion is a clear and unmistakable requirement for an established, educated and robust Navy Space Cadre. Less concrete is direction provided regarding Navy requirements or benefits to be gained from internal acquisition and operation of space systems."

65 "Ingrain Cultural Change: Harvest space-related best practices from Naval Space Campaign lessons learned and institutionalize them through doctrine and policy."

66 "The president authorized a new national space policy on August 31, 2006 that establishes overarching national policy that governs the conduct of U.S. space activities."

67 "The results of this experiment have not been officially released, but preliminary indications point to notable successes for the implementation of space effects at the operational level, and validation of the concept of a 'space-enabled staff.'"

68 "These failings in policy pose an impediment to the success of the Navy Space Campaign. The lack of guidance and direction, in conjunction with platitudes regarding network centric warfare and party-line rhetoric, needs to be addressed and reevaluated by senior Navy leadership. In order to assure success in current and future Navy Space operations, leadership must jump-start space requirements and processes with a critical revision of Naval Space policy."

69 "Knowledge of how space effects get to the CSG and ESG is critical to ensuring warfighters have required space effects."

70. CSG-8/IKESG has benefited greatly from our journey as the fleet EA for space. We are smarter towards our use of space capabilities and better recognize our vulnerabilities in that regard as well. As such we are better prepared to prevail in conflict.

71. "Commander, IKESG could say with confidence that every bit of space capability available was brought to bear in support of designated operational events."

72. "Good, bad or otherwise, the Navy Space Campaign is underway, and only through sound decision making and aggressive leadership will the Navy space community be able to navigate through the troubled waters that lie ahead."

74. "The creation of the Navy Space Cadre has been established in a parallel but unequal effort with the Air Force, Army and Marine Corps Space Cadres. The differences among the service efforts in constructing their organizations of 'space experts' is instructive as to the assessed cost-benefit relation that each branch assigns to its use of space, and relative leadership understanding of the impact of space effects."

75. "Only with senior-level leadership, when properly managed and with the right priorities will U.S. space programs both deserve and attract the funding that is required."

76. "To ensure the needed talent and experience, the Department of Defense, the Intelligence Community and the nation as a whole must place a high priority on intensifying investments in career development, education and training to develop and sustain a cadre of highly competent and motivated military and civilian space professionals."

77. "The Air Force and Marine Corps have taken significant actions to develop and manage their space cadres; however, the Army's and Navy's actions have been limited because these two services do not have clear goals and objectives for their space cadres or focal points designated to manage the cadres."

78. "The Navy decision to forego a specific community and designation for space qualified personnel resulted in a dilution of institutional support for the mission, absence of quantifiable processes for the organization, and absence of appropriate funding. Only in the Navy are space-trained personnel not routinely assigned to space-related positions or belong to a Space Cadre that has the authority to assign personnel to specific positions."

79. "Remediation of problems caused by this lack of satellite operator warfighting acumen must occur on the ground, usually in theater, through the efforts of experienced space products users like Army FA-40s and Marine Corps Space Cadre members."

80. "The rapid response to the GAO report on the part of the Secretary of the Air Force is indicative of the seriousness which that service (Air Force) approaches space planning and policy. Indeed, the 2004 GAO report is as, if not more, critical of shortcomings in U.S. Navy and Army implementation of Space Cadre planning and execution as it is of the Department of Defense as a whole."

82. "The Air Force identifies space as a core competency of the service in general, and is responsible for the full spectrum of space-related endeavors, from engineering design and construction of space systems, to the full spectrum of strategic, operational and tactical utilization of those assets."

83. "Although not specifically branded by the Government Accountability Office as the DoD component with the most lackluster space-qualified personnel management system, one of the implications of the 2004 GAO report was that the Navy had the farthest to go in developing an effective Space Cadre."

84. "Centralization of organization and planning for the Navy Space Cadre, an issue identified as a major topic heading in the August 2004 GAO report, achieved an obvious high priority in the Navy's space professional efforts."

85   "To date, all three of the Naval officers that have served as the Space Cadre Advisor have been high-profile, highly-educated, proven performers who brought ambition and drive to the otherwise stagnant Navy efforts at codifying the requirements and responsibilities of the Navy Space Cadre."

86   The Navy Space Cadre Human Capital Strategy does not, however, address the following issues – issues of great import when viewed against the background of the fully established, mission-oriented Space Cadre of the Air Force, and the revised 2006 National Space Policy: • Articulation of required Core Competencies for Navy Space personnel. • Composition of a list of "Best Practices" for the Navy Space community. • Establishment of a list of billets critical to the Navy Space community. • Construction and validation of a Navy Space Cadre Professional Certification.

87   "All of these measures are shortfalls noted within the Navy Space Human Capital Strategy, identifying them as clearly within the radar horizon of the community leadership, but beyond the sensor range of senior Navy leadership. Additionally, these shortfalls in the Navy's strategy are notable in that they have all been solved by other services."

88   "Success of naval operations is dependent on the capabilities of national, DoD and commercial space support. It is imperative that the Navy develops a significant cadre, comprised of the URL and RL communities, that is competent in relating the areas of operations, requirements, development and acquisition to space. Members of this cadre may have atypical career paths because of specialized education, training and assignments outside of the Navy. This cadre will continue to represent the Navy in mid-level and senior joint billets, as well as be assigned to Navy billets in direct support of space requirements and acquisition. When selecting the best and fully qualified officers to meet the needs of the..."

89   "Navy, you must view the quality of performance of offices in the Space Cadre as having weight equal to that ordinarily given to the quality of performance of other members of their respective communities who have followed more traditional career paths."

90   "Although these AQD codes are in place in the Navy personnel system and Officer Service Records, it is unclear as to whether the addition of these codes is sufficient to identify exceptionally qualified Space Cadre personnel for promotion."

91   "The threat posed by potential elimination of Navy presence in shore billets, and especially joint shore billets, cannot be overstated. As the Navy influence in space systems and operations has waned, the Space Cadre personnel filling positions where they have ready contact with members of the greater DoD space community are the only remaining leverage that the Navy has to apply to fulfill needs supported by space systems. Without input provided by operational, military Navy space personnel, Navy needs for space systems will be unfilled, as the requirements and acquisition process for these systems proceeds."

92   "The resulting uphill battle in attempting to provide commanders with the information, capabilities and services they desire at the operational level will prove a frustration to both commanders and operators alike. Worse, the lack of functional expertise and resulting weak job performance will diminish the credibility of the Space Cadre as a whole, exacerbating the problem of leadership ambivalence with regard to space-provided capabilities."

93   "In the typical shipboard environment, the officer's focus of effort must be on their primary duty. Collateral duties, by nature, are secondary to the primary job assignment. For this reason, space subspecialty coding for particular billets at sea is generally a paper

tiger, with only as much bite as an individual has spare time to focus on that secondary mission."

94 *"The recognition and success that the CSG-8 experiment achieved can be traced to the uncommon efforts of one individual on that staff. In much the same way as recent refinement and development of the Navy Space Cadre can be traced to the current Space Cadre Advisor, the CSG-8 Air Operations Officer, a Space Cadre member functioned as the Deputy, Space Warfare Commander to the Commander, Carrier Strike Group 8. The status of this position, a collateral duty as noted above, was significantly elevated for the purpose of the Naval Space Campaign effort, yet the officer assigned to the position continued to perform both his 'warfare specialty' job as a primary assignment and his Space Cadre job at superlative levels."*

95 *"That the recommendation is internally consistent with the Navy Space Cadre Human Capital Strategy does not, however, invalidate it – one of the stated goals of the Strategy is to 'Gain senior leadership support throughout the Navy', and that leadership support can come only with a point of focus within the operational staff that simultaneously provides space effects and can promote the cause of the Navy Space Cadre."*

96 *"The Air Force identifies 7,195 space positions for their personnel base, representing a 97% utilization rate for their Space Cadre. The Army has a similar utilization rate for its Space Cadre. In contrast, because of the "cross-community" nature of the Navy Space Cadre, more than half of Navy officers with space training and qualifications are employed in jobs that are unrelated to space and have no requirement for the training these personnel possess. Across the DoD, only 315 positions for Navy Officer Space Cadre members exist, providing a 40% utilization rate for this community. This gross mismatch of availability of space-trained personnel with the number of space-related jobs under Navy control is a necessity under the current Navy Space Cadre "cross*

97 *"The evidence clearly indicates that highly trained personnel with substantial space expertise placed in positions where they can affect leverage on national space efforts promote the cause of the Navy Space Cadre, Navy Space Campaign, Sea Power 21 and the national interest."*

98 *"Without a steering force applied to the institution and a re-assessment of what space missions are of critical value to the Navy, the remaining corporate knowledge inherent in the Navy's scattered space organizations and nascent Space Cadre is likely to fragment and disappear entirely."*

99 *"A much more appropriate business structure to accomplish the missions of satellite operation and control is to consolidate all of these functions under one organization, with appropriate representation from the various service stakeholders. Consolidation can produce cost reductions through the use of shared administration and overhead, and single-entity operation of space systems reduces the internal command complexities inherent in service-specific space operations organizations."*

100 *"The squadron operates and maintains communications-computer systems establishing real-time global connectivity to more than 170 satellites comprising the Global Positioning System, Defense Meteorological Satellite Program, Defense Satellite Program, Defense Satellite Communications System, Milstar, Fleet Satellite Communications System, Ultra High Frequency Follow-On System, North Atlantic Treaty Organization, Defense Advanced Research Program Agency and test system satellites through the $8.2 billion Air Force Satellite Control Network."*

102 *"To eliminate the redundancies and overhead intrinsic to the fragmented satellite control structure, the Navy should divest itself of the missions performed by NAVSOC and*

	transfer its remaining satellite operation and control responsibilities to the Air Force's 50th Space Wing."
103	"The United States Navy and Marine Corps must maintain their ability to tactically exploit the capabilities provided by space systems and participate in all appropriate aspects of the changed NSS environment in order to function as an integrated member of the Nation's joint warfighting team."
104	Elimination of the Navy component of the satellite command and control function is an almost trivial undertaking, and can assist in a tidy centralization of satellite operation efforts. The equipment, infrastructure and operational presence required to fly and operate the NAVSOC satellite inventory already exists at the Air Force's 14th Air Force and subordinate 50th Space Wing. Additionally, from an organizational structure standpoint, NAVSOC currently falls under the tactical control (TACON) of the Joint Space Operations Center (JSpOC), another organization subordinate to Commander, 14th Air Force. Years of command cooperation and careful definition and nurturing of command relationships could allow for the addition of Navy representation at the 50th Space Wing and 14th Air Force to ensure Navy requirements
106	"Clearly, when contrasted with the massive volume of Air Force Satellite Control Network daily events (more than 10,000 per day), the small quantity of systems and contact events the NAVSOC manages pose no impediment to the Air Force absorbing these functions."
108	"In contrast, incorporation of NAVSOC missions into the Air Force satellite C^2 architecture eliminates a non-core business from the Navy's slate of missions, centralizes responsibility and authority for the operation of space systems, simplifies funding and administration and eliminates redundancy."
109	Without consideration of the NetOps and Information Operations missions, the space-coordination function, embodied in a sub-unit of the NNWC MOC called the "Space Cell" is completely superfluous and redundant to the Joint Space Operations Center (JSpOC). Navy forces reachback for space support, planning and effects through the Space Cell introduces a completely unnecessary layer to the space support hierarchy and re-directs information flow through an additional, needless loop. (Refer to Figure 5, page 49). The NNWC MOC Space Cell is critically dependent upon space-related information provided and brokered by the JSpOC, and serves only as a conduit and middleman to transfer that information to afloat forces. The Space Cell, upon receiving requests
110	"The logical and proper information structure eliminates the NNWC Space Cell from the loop, with maritime users reaching directly to the JSpOC for space resource assistance. To allay the concerns of the Navy user regarding defense of Navy-specific space requirements, manning adjustments at the JSpOC should be considered, with increased numbers and insertion of appropriate expertise sourced from the Navy Space Cadre. This solution poses a win-win from the perspective of both the Air Force space operations community and the Navy Space Cadre, providing needed personnel for manning, cross-cultural training and experience for the Space Cadre, and multi-service legitimacy for the JSpOC as operational usage increases."
112	"The effort for design and acquisition of MUOS is lauded as a high-quality acquisition program amidst a panoply of spectacular failures in space systems acquisition."
113	"Today, bandwidth requirements shipboard far exceed the ability of UHF to deliver data. Instead, the disadvantaged mobile user, typically assessed as troops on the ground, is the intended beneficiary of the 'last-mile' MUOS system."
114	"In the same way that the various services should turn to the Air Force as the service provider for satellite operations and bandwidth, so should the Navy relinquish its

	development and acquisition of satellite systems to the Air Force. With 'historical imperative' as the primary rationale for continuing to field and acquire satellites, the Navy needs to divest itself of this non-core operation."
115	"While the shift of programmatic and acquisition responsibilities to the Air Force represents a loss of funds to the Navy, recovery of the human resources from PEO Space and PMW-146 presents an excellent opportunity for the strengthening of both the Navy Space Cadre as well as the real historical core competency of the Navy's space efforts – scientific research and technology development."
116	"NRL, the Navy's single, integrated Corporate Laboratory, provides the Navy with a broad foundation of in-house expertise from scientific through advanced development activity."
117	"Without the burden of needing to support Navy-specific acquisition, personnel and efforts could be used to fulfill Navy needs in space at the technology development level rather than the systems deployment level. Use of this extensive intellectual talent pool with relief from the political considerations and Byzantine maneuvering of systems acquisition permits more productive research, with corresponding improvements in systems refinement and development time."
118	"Returning the Navy to active participation, funding and use of its own premier space systems research and development organization is a crucial step in centralizing and simplifying the complex mish-mash of space systems requirements articulation, capabilities experimentation and systems design and development. Through a renaissance in S&T, and recognition of that function as a core competency of the Navy's space efforts, representation of the Navy's needs in space can be more clearly articulated to organizations acting as service providers."
119	"Revitalization of the role of the NRL and NCST as the 'center of excellence' for Navy Space provides not only an organizational hub for the ad-hocracy that describes the larger Navy Space organization, but also supports Department of Defense requirements to maintain space skills in an expert cadre."
120	"Without clear and unambiguous requirements definition on the part of the Navy for future space systems, participation in future conflicts will be restricted by unmet needs."
121	n/a
122	"The time has come for the Navy to relinquish its redundant operational control of communication satellites and re-focus on science and technology research. Secondly, current efforts by NETWARCOM and senior Navy leadership to establish a solid Navy Space Cadre fall short when compared to other services' efforts. The future success of Navy space is dependent on the growth and empowerment of a vigorous Navy Space Cadre. Finally, to ensure the maximum effectiveness of future Navy space efforts, the Navy must redefine its role in the acquisition process by eliminating the PEO Space Systems office, to include PMW-146, and reinvest in the NRL, ensuring continuation of necessary S&T research and advancements. These proposed restructuring efforts can pave the way to the realization of the full potential of the
123	"Additional clarity in the Navy space doctrinal library regarding an implementation strategy and consolidated Navy space architecture is needed, as well as leadership involvement and guidance in the joint space environment."
124	"Space power provides military leaders, operators, and planners with enormous force-enhancement effects that multiply joint combat effectiveness in prosecuting theater campaigns. Space systems significantly improve friendly forces' ability to strike at the enemy's heart or COGs, paralyzing an adversary to allow land, sea, and air forces to achieve rapid dominance of the battlespace."

125   "The unlimited potential of space has captured the imagination of generations of Americans. Novelists, scientists, filmmakers, and military theorists have all endeavored to address the latent promise of the 'ultimate high ground'."

126   "Undisputed combat space power is drawing near, and the United States may be on the brink of unleashing decisive military space operations, ushering in the era of a separate space force. The reality is that, as in the evolution of airpower, the true potential of a nation's military space power will come to fruition only when a separate space force is created, complete with its own space-competent leadership, organization, doctrine, theory, policy, and resources."

127   "Leadership in modern military space efforts is less about an organization's ability to field equipment and orbital systems, and more about effective and rapid policy implementation, institutional focus and clear, concise requirements definition. In recent years, the Navy has fallen short in these undertakings. Senior Navy leadership seems to perceive space-related missions as an on-demand service, without a grasp of the complexities inherent in the operation of the required architectures. Policy and doctrine, though enunciated at the appropriate levels, lacks clarity and specifics and provides insufficient guidance for the naval planner of space systems."

128   "with a strong investment in its space cadre and redirected efforts supporting fundamental science and technology, that future promises to be as bright as the historical achievements of past."

141   "SEA POWER 21 defines a Navy with three fundamental concepts: SEA SHIELD, SEA STRIKE, and the SEA BASE, enabled by FORCEnet. Respectively, they enhance America's ability to project offensive power, defensive assurance, and operational independence around the globe."

143   "Joint Warfighting Space brings space effects directly to the Joint Force Commander."

NAVAL POSTGRADUATE SCHOOL

MONTEREY, CALIFORNIA

THESIS

A MODEST PROPOSAL: FOR PREVENTING SPACE OPERATIONS FROM BEING A BURDEN TO THE NAVY, AND FOR MAKING THE SPACE CADRE BENEFICIAL TO THE COMMUNITY

by

Paul V. Bandini
Andrew R. Dittmer

September 2007

Thesis Advisor: Charles M. Racoosin
Second Reader: William J. Welch

Approved for public release; distribution is unlimited

THIS PAGE INTENTIONALLY LEFT BLANK

REPORT DOCUMENTATION PAGE			Form Approved OMB No. 0704-0188
Public reporting burden for this collection of information is estimated to average 1 hour per response, including the time for reviewing instruction, searching existing data sources, gathering and maintaining the data needed, and completing and reviewing the collection of information. Send comments regarding this burden estimate or any other aspect of this collection of information, including suggestions for reducing this burden, to Washington headquarters Services, Directorate for Information Operations and Reports, 1215 Jefferson Davis Highway, Suite 1204, Arlington, VA 22202-4302, and to the Office of Management and Budget, Paperwork Reduction Project (0704-0188) Washington DC 20503.			
1. AGENCY USE ONLY *(Leave blank)*	**2. REPORT DATE** September 2007	**3. REPORT TYPE AND DATES COVERED** Master's Thesis	
4. TITLE AND SUBTITLE A Modest Proposal: for Preventing Space Operations from Being a Burden to the Navy, and for Making the Space Cadre Beneficial to the Community.		**5. FUNDING NUMBERS**	
6. AUTHOR(S) LCDR Paul V. Bandini, LCDR Andrew R. Dittmer			
7. PERFORMING ORGANIZATION NAME(S) AND ADDRESS(ES) Naval Postgraduate School Monterey, CA 93943-5000		**8. PERFORMING ORGANIZATION REPORT NUMBER**	
9. SPONSORING /MONITORING AGENCY NAME(S) AND ADDRESS(ES) N/A		**10. SPONSORING/MONITORING AGENCY REPORT NUMBER**	
11. SUPPLEMENTARY NOTES The views expressed in this thesis are those of the author and do not reflect the official policy or position of the Department of Defense or the U.S. Government.			
12a. DISTRIBUTION / AVAILABILITY STATEMENT Approved for public release; distribution is unlimited.		**12b. DISTRIBUTION CODE** A	
13. ABSTRACT (maximum 200 words) U.S. Navy efforts in implementing Department of Defense policy guidance for the effective integration of space capabilities and effects consist of a variety of multi-pronged and disjointed efforts. Lack of clear direction in analysis and identification of current and future requirements for space-related capabilities presents a hazard to implementation of the tenants of Sea Power 21 and Navy participation in future conflicts.

This work proposes an alternative construct for the organization and utilization of Navy space resources against the backdrop of requirements levied by the 2001 U.S. Commission to Assess National Security Space Management and Organizations and resulting Department of Defense Directive 5101.2, DoD Executive Agent for Space.

In order to accomplish its mission, the Navy must establish a clear focus of effort, consolidate and formalize space-related human capital and divest itself of space-specific undertakings not related to core functions. This thesis establishes arguments to propose that the United States Navy relinquish development, acquisition and satellite operations tasks to another service or agency, and invest in appropriately leveraging space assets through the professionalization and promotion of a robust, educated, experienced and capable Navy Space Cadre. | | | |
14. SUBJECT TERMS: Executive Agent for Space, Navy Space Cadre, Human Capital Strategy, Sea Power 21, Naval Network Warfare Command (NETWARCOM), Navy Space Operations Command (NAVSOC), Network Information Operations and Space Center (NIOSC), Naval Research Laboratory (NRL), Naval Center for Space Technology (NCST), Carrier Strike Group (CSG).		**15. NUMBER OF PAGES** 155	
		16. PRICE CODE	
17. SECURITY CLASSIFICATION OF REPORT Unclassified	**18. SECURITY CLASSIFICATION OF THIS PAGE** Unclassified	**19. SECURITY CLASSIFICATION OF ABSTRACT** Unclassified	**20. LIMITATION OF ABSTRACT** UU

NSN 7540-01-280-5500

Standard Form 298 (Rev. 2-89)
Prescribed by ANSI Std. 239-18

i

THIS PAGE INTENTIONALLY LEFT BLANK

Approved for public release; distribution is unlimited.

A MODEST PROPOSAL: FOR PREVENTING SPACE OPERATIONS FROM BEING A BURDEN TO THE NAVY, AND FOR MAKING THE SPACE CADRE BENEFICIAL TO THE COMMUNITY

Paul V. Bandini
Lieutenant Commander, United States Navy
B.S., Texas A&M University, 1996

Andrew R. Dittmer
Lieutenant Commander, United States Navy
B.S., United States Naval Academy, 1997

Submitted in partial fulfillment of the
requirements for the degree of

MASTER OF SCIENCE IN SPACE SYSTEMS OPERATIONS

from the

NAVAL POSTGRADUATE SCHOOL
September 2007

Author: Paul V. Bandini

                Andrew R. Dittmer

Approved by: Charles M. Racoosin
                Thesis Advisor

                William J. Welch
                Second Reader

                Rudy Panholzer
                Chairman, Space Systems Academic Group

THIS PAGE INTENTIONALLY LEFT BLANK

ABSTRACT

U.S. Navy efforts in implementing Department of Defense policy guidance for the effective integration of space capabilities and effects consist of a variety of multi-pronged and disjointed efforts. Lack of clear direction in analysis and identification of current and future requirements for space-related capabilities presents a hazard to implementation of the tenants of Sea Power 21 and Navy participation in future conflicts.

This work proposes an alternative construct for the organization and utilization of Navy space resources against the backdrop of requirements levied by the 2001 U.S. Commission to Assess National Security Space Management and Organizations and resulting Department of Defense Directive 5101.2, DoD Executive Agent for Space.

In order to accomplish its mission, the Navy must establish a clear focus of effort, consolidate and formalize space-related human capital and divest itself of space-specific undertakings not related to core functions. This thesis establishes arguments to propose that the United States Navy relinquish development, acquisition and satellite operations tasks to another service or agency, and invest in appropriately leveraging space assets through the professionalization and promotion of a robust, educated, experienced and capable Navy Space Cadre.

THIS PAGE INTENTIONALLY LEFT BLANK

TABLE OF CONTENTS

I. HISTORY 1
    A. THE BEGINNINGS OF PRACTICAL ROCKETRY 1
    B. WORLD WAR II DEVELOPMENTS..3
    C. POST-WAR CUTBACKS AND COMPETITION..3
    D. THE SOVIET THREAT AND MILITARY PROGRAM RESURGENCE..6
    E. NASA, ARPA, AND THE MILITARY BRAIN DRAIN..........................7
    F. MILITARY PROGRAMS PRIOR TO 1961..9
    G. FIRST ESTABLISHMENT OF THE "EXECUTIVE AGENT FOR SPACE" 11
    H. SPACE PROGRAM DIVERGENCE IN THE MILITARY SERVICES...13
    I. ESTABLISHMENT OF THE UNITED STATES SPACE COMMAND AND GROWTH OF NAVAL SPACE..14
    J. THE CONTESTED MISSION AREA AND NATIONAL SPACE REORGANIZATION..17

II. SIGNIFICANT DEFINITIONS 25
    A. ORGANIZATIONS 25
        1. January 11, 2001 U.S. Commission to Assess National Security Space Management and Organizations (2001 Space Commission) 25
        2. Naval Network Warfare Command (NETWARCOM)...................26
        3. NETWARCOM (NNWC) Maritime Operations Center (MOC) Space Cell...27
        4. Naval Satellite Operations Center (NAVSOC) 27
        5. Maritime Headquarters with Maritime Operations Center (MHQ-MOC)...29
        6. Carrier Strike Group (CSG) 29
        7. Joint Space Operations Center (JSpOC)...30
        8. Government Accountability Office (GAO)..30
        9. Space and Naval Warfare Systems Command (SPAWAR)............31
        10. Program Executive Officer (PEO) Space Systems...........................31
        11. Navy Communications Satellite Program Office (PMW-146).......32
        12. National Reconnaissance Office (NRO) 33
        13. Naval Research Laboratory (NRL) 33
        14. Navy Center for Space Technology (NCST).....................................34
    B. CONCEPTS 34
        1. Sea Power 21..34
        2. Coordinating Authority..35
        3. Space Authority...36
        4. Space Coordinating Authority (SCA)...36
        5. Joint Warfighting Space (JWS)...37

			6.	Space Effects and Space Effects Packages 38

III. U.S. NAVY SPACE CAMPAIGN 39
    A. POLICY 39
        1. Background and Current Policies 39
            a. SECNAVINST 5400.39C (April 6, 2004) 40
            b. CJCSI 6250.01B (May 28, 2004) 41
            c. *Navy Space Cadre Human Capital Strategy (December 2004)* 41
            d. OPNAVINST 5400.43 (May 20, 2005) 42
            e. *Naval Space Campaign Plan 2005-2007 (November 13, 2005)* 43
            f. *U.S. National Space Policy (August 31, 2006)* 45
        2. Positive Aspects of the Navy's Space Policy 45
        3. Negative Aspects of the Navy's Space Policy 46
    B. NAVY SPACE CAMPAIGN COMMAND AND CONTROL CONSTRUCT 47
    C. FUTURE ENDEAVORS 50

IV. NAVY SPACE CADRE 53
    A. ORIGIN 53
        1. DoD-wide Policy 53
        2. The Navy Response. 55
    B. COMPARISONS -- OTHER DOD SPACE CADRE 57
        1. Government Accountability Office and the Executive Agent for Space 59
        2. The Good 59
        3. …the Bad… 61
        4. …and the Ugly. 62
    C. GROWTH AND MATURATION OF THE NAVY SPACE CADRE. 63
        1. Navy Space Human Capital Strategy 63
        2. Navy Space Cadre Advisor 64
        3. Shortfalls 65
    D. CONTINUANCE AND PROMOTION OF THE NAVY SPACE CADRE 67
        1. Promotion Board Precept Language 67
        2. Additional Qualification Designations and Subspecialty Codes 68
    E. CURRENT SPACE CADRE PERSONNEL ASSIGNMENT EFFORTS 70
        1. The Sea – Shore Rotation Conundrum 70
        2. Seagoing Space Cadre Support and the CSG-8 Space Team 71
        3. Navy Space Cadre in the Joint and National Environment 74

V. NAVY SPACE: CORE BUSINESSES AND OUTSOURCING 77
    A. REDUNDANCY IN THE REALM OF CONTROL 78
    B. NAVY SATELLITE SYSTEMS OPERATIONS 81
        1. Facilities & Locations 84

2. Personnel 84
3. Operations 85
4. Benefits 86
C. NAVY OPERATIONAL SPACE SUPPORT 87
D. NAVY SATELLITE SYSTEMS ACQUISITION 90
1. Background and Specifics 91
2. True Acquisition Reform… 92
E. REINVORGATION OF NAVY SPACE S&T AND UTILIZATION OF THE NAVAL RESEARCH LABORATORY 94
1. Mission & Focus of Effort 95
2. Recovery of Capabilities 96
3. Human Capital Re-Use 97
F. SELLING THE FARM…AND BUYING A NEW ONE 99

VI. FINAL CONCLUSIONS AND RECOMMENDATIONS 101
A. THESIS SUMMARY 101
B. FURTHER EXPLORATION 103
1. Navy Space Officer (NSO) 104
2. United States Space Force 105
C. CONCLUSION 106

APPENDIX: SIGNIFICANT DEFINITIONS 109
A. ORGANIZATIONS 109
1. January 11, 2001 U.S. Commission to Assess National Security Space Management and Organizations (2001 Space Commission) 109
2. Naval Network Warfare Command 110
3. Network, Information Operations, and Space Center Space Cell 111
4. Naval Satellite Operations Center (NAVSOC) 113
5. Maritime Headquarters with Maritime Operations Center (MHQ-MOC) 113
6. Carrier Strike Group (CSG) 114
7. Joint Space Operations Center (JSpOC) 115
8. Government Accountability Office (GAO) 115
9. Space and Naval Warfare Systems Command (SPAWAR) 116
10. Program Executive Office (PEO) Space Systems 116
11. Navy Communications Satellite Program Office (PMW-146) 117
12. National Reconnaissance Office (NRO) 117
13. Naval Research Laboratories (NRL) 118
14. Navy Center for Space Technology (NCST) 119
B. CONCEPTS 120
1. Sea Power 21 120
2. Coordinating Authority 121
3. Space Authority 122
4. Space Coordinating Authority (SCA) 122
5. Joint Warfighting Space 122

| | 6. | Space Effects and Space Effects Packages | 123 |

LIST OF REFERENCES 125

INITIAL DISTRIBUTION LIST 133

LIST OF FIGURES

Figure 1.	NAVSOC Satellite Operations Locations	28
Figure 2.	PEO Space Systems in the Context of Space Systems Acquisition	32
Figure 3.	Joint Warfighter Space Operational Vision	37
Figure 4.	C^2 Historical Flow Chart for the Naval Satellite Operations Center	48
Figure 5.	CSG-8 C^2 Space Effects Operational Flow Chart modified by authors to reflect Navy Space Cadre Representation Requirements	49
Figure 6.	Space Systems Operations Subspecialty Historical Fit and Fill Rates.	65
Figure 7.	In-Zone Promotion Rates for Navy Space Cadre Personnel	68
Figure 8.	A Snap Shot of Daily Operations at NAVSOC	85
Figure 9.	Naval Satellite Operations Center Operations Data Flow Diagram	113
Figure 10.	Standard CSG Profile	114
Figure 11.	Program Executive Office Space Systems Organizational Chart	116
Figure 12.	PMW-146 Communications Satellite Programs Office Organizational Chart	117
Figure 13.	Sea Power 21 Diagram	121

THIS PAGE INTENTIONALLY LEFT BLANK

LIST OF TABLES

Table 1.	Air Force Percentage of DoD Space Capabilities.	21
Table 2.	NAVSOC Functional Control by Location	28
Table 3.	NAVSOC Manning Breakdown as of 2006	84

THIS PAGE INTENTIONALLY LEFT BLANK

LIST OF SYMBOLS, ACRONYMS, AND ABBREVIATIONS

AF	Air Force
AFB	Air Force Base
AFDD	Air Force Doctrine Document
AFSC	Air Force Space Command
AFSCN	Air Force Satellite Control Network
AOC	Air Operations Center
AOE	Combat Supply Ship
AOR	Area of Responsibility
APL	Applied Physics Laboratory
AQD	Additional Qualification Designator
ARPA	Advanced Research Projects Agency
ASN(RDA)	Assistant Secretary of the Navy for Research, Development, and Acquisition
ATO	Air Tasking Order
C2	Command and Control
C3I	Command, Control, Communications and Intelligence
C4ISR	Command, Control, Communications, and Computers, Intelligence, Surveillance, and Reconnaissance
CCDR	Component Commander
CDR	Commander
CDRJSO	Commander, Joint Space Operations
CENTCOM	Central Command
CFACC	Combined Forces Air Component Commander
CG	Guided Missile Cruiser
CIA	Central Intelligence Agency
CINC	Commander-in-Chief
CJCSI	Chairman of the Joint Chiefs of Staff Instruction

CMC	Commandant Marine Corps
CNO	Chief of Naval Operations
COA	Course of Action
COMAFFOR	Commander of Air Force Forces
COMM	Communications
CONOPS	Concept of Operation
CSG	Carrier Strike Group
CVN	Aircraft Carrier
DARPA	Defense Advanced research Projects Agency
DDG	Guided Missile Destroyer
DNRO	Director of the National Reconnaissance Office
DoD	Department of Defense
DODD	Department of Defense Directive
DOD SA	Department of Defense Space Architecture
DON	Department of the Navy
DSCS	Defense Satellite Communications System
DSP	Defense Support Program
DUSD Space	Deputy Undersecretary of Defense for Space
EA	Executive Agent
EEHF	Enhanced Extremely High Frequency
EHF	Extremely High Frequency
EMI	Electro-Magnetic Interference
ESG	Expeditionary Strike Group
FEP	Extremely High Frequency Package
FFC	Fleet Forces Command
FLTSATCOM	Fleet Satellite Communications
FM	Field Manual
FY	Fiscal Year
GAO	Government Accountability Office
GBS	Global Broadcast Service
GEOSAT	Geodetic Satellite

GFO	Geodetic Satellite Follow-On
GIG	Global Information Grid
GPS	Global Positioning System
GWOT	Global War on Terrorism
HCRS	Human Capital Resource Strategy
HCS	Human Capital Strategy
IC	Intelligence Community
ICBM	Intercontinental Ballistic Missile
IKESG	USS EISENHOWER Strike Group
IO	Information Operations
IRBM	Intermediate Range Ballistic Missile
ISO	In Support Of
IT	Information Technology
JATO	Jet Assisted Take-Off
JCS	Joint Chiefs of Staff
JFC	Joint Forces Commander
JFACC	Joint Forces Air Component Commander
JFCC	Joint Forces Component Commander
JFMCC	Joint Forces Maritime Component Commander
JOA	Joint Operations Area
JP	Joint Publication
JSMB	Joint Space Management Board
JSpOC	Joint Space Operations Center
JSTO	Joint Space Tasking Order
JTAGS	Joint Tactical Ground Station
JTF	Joint Task Force
JWS	Joint Warfighting Space
LEASAT	Leased Satellite
LOFTI	Low-Frequency Traps-Ionosphere
MDA	Maritime Domain Awareness
MHQ	Maritime Head Quarters

MIT	Massachusetts Institute of Technology
MOC	Maritime Operations Center
MSEL	Master Scenario Event List
MUOS	Mobile User Objective System
NASA	National Aeronautics and Space Administration
NATO	North Atlantic Treaty Organization
NAVCENT	Naval Central Command
NAVELEXSYSCOM	Navy Electronic Systems Command
NAVSOC	Naval Satellite Operations Center
NAVSPACECOM	Naval Space Command
NCC	Naval Component Commander
NCST	Navy Center for Space Technology
NETOPS	Network Operations
NETWARCOM	Naval Network Warfare Command
NGA	National Geospatial-Intelligence Agency
NIMS	Navy Ionospheric Monitoring System
NIOSC	Network, Information Operations, and Space Center
NMET	Naval Mission Essential Task
NNWC	Naval Network Warfare Command
NRL	Naval Research Laboratory
NRO	National Reconnaissance Office
NSCN	Naval Satellite Control Network
NSMS	National Strategy on Maritime Security
NSS	National Security Space
NSSI	National Security Space Institute
NSSAP	National Security Space Acquisition Policy
OLW	Operational-Level of War
ONR	Office of Naval Research
OPCON	Operational Control
OPNAV	Office of the Chief of Naval Operations

OPNAVINST	Office of the Chief of Naval Operations Instruction
OSD	Office of the Secretary of Defense
PDOP	Position Dilution of Precision
PEO	Program Executive Office
PMW-146	Communications Satellite Program Office
RAND (R&D)	Research and Development
RL	Restricted Line
SATCOM	Satellite Communications
SCA	Space Coordinating Authority
S/C	Space Craft
SCS	Space Communications Squadron
SECNAVINST	Secretary of the Navy Instruction
SED	Spacecraft Engineering Department
SEP	Space Effects Package
SGS	Space and Global Strike
SHF	Super High Frequency
SLEP	Service life Extension Program
SOC	Space Operations Center
SOLRAD	Solar Radiation
SOPS	Space Operations Squadron
SPAWAR	Space and Naval Warfare Systems Command
SPINS	Special Instructions
SSA	Space Situational Awareness
SSC	SPAWAR Systems Center
SSDD	Space Systems Development Department
SSFA	SPAWAR Space Field Activity
SSN	Fast Attack Submarine
STO	Space Tasking Order
SURCAL	Surveillance Calibration
SW	Space Wing

T&C	Telemetry and Command
TACAIR	Tactical Air Forces
TACON	Tactical Control
TCA	Transformational Communications Architecture
TENCAP	Tactical Exploitation of National Capabilities
TFO	TRANSIT Follow-on
TLAM	Tomahawk Land Attack Missile
TLM	Telemetry
TT&C	Tracking, Telemetry and Command
TTP	Turnaround Training Plans
TYCOM	Type Commander
UCP	Unified Command Plan
UFO	Ultra High Frequency Follow-On
UHF	Ultra High Frequency
UNAAF	Unified Action Armed Forces
URL	Unrestricted Line
USSPACECOM	U.S. Space Command
USSR	Union of Soviet Socialist Republic
USSTRATCOM	U.S. Strategic Command

I. HISTORY

Present day issues regarding national policy, doctrine and utilization of U.S. space assets have their roots in a complex history of inter-service competition and a half-century of rapidly changing global political environments. This chapter is intended to provide a historical perspective for subsequent commentary on resource utilization in the national space arena. U.S. Navy efforts in space date to the very earliest experimentation in the field, and the people and personalities involved are among the most influential in the world. Proud tradition, however, like royalty and empire, has a tendency to become exclusive, diseased and weakened. Apropos of the gradual collapse of the Roman Empire, the house of Navy Space has slid into disrepair from its heights in the 1940s and 1980s. Ahead remain decisions on the Navy's involvement in space, but in the past lies the following history:

A. THE BEGINNINGS OF PRACTICAL ROCKETRY

Space systems development in the U.S. prior to the end of World War II was largely conducted by the Army and Navy on an ad-hoc basis, with the personality and genius of specific luminaries providing the foundation and direction for the service programs. Practical work that led to the U.S.'s ability to operate in the space environment began in 1926, with the efforts of Dr. Robert Goddard. Goddard proved, during work between 1912 and 1926 on liquid-fueled rockets, that they would produce usable thrust in the vacuum of space. Until his experiments, scientists were in wide disagreement as to whether propulsion in space was possible without a medium to push against. Goddard's testing and design of liquid-fueled rockets captured the attention of a group of German scientists when in 1920 he published a paper for the Smithsonian Institution entitled "*A Method of Reaching Extreme Altitudes.*" These German scientists, in 1927, founded the German Rocket Society (Vercin für Raumschiffart – Society for Space Travel), which was subsumed into the German Army's rocket program in 1931.[1]

---

[1] Lynn Jenner. *Dr. Robert H. Goddard: American Rocket Pioneer.* December 2004. http://www.nasa.gov/centers/goddard/about/dr_goddard.html. May 2007.

Despite the warm reception that Goddard's 1920 paper received in Europe, and specifically Germany, the popular press in the U.S. lampooned his efforts and ridiculed and misquoted his comments hypothesizing the possibility of launching a rocket to the moon. The negative press had the effect of damaging Goddard's credibility with the mainstream American scientific and military establishment, and despite repeated offers of service to the government, he was turned down multiple times in the years before World War II.

Following the less-than-supportive reception of "*A Method of Reaching Extreme Altitudes*", Dr. Goddard found financing and support from Daniel Guggenheim, a former naval aviator. With Guggenheim's patronage, Goddard constructed an experimental rocket pad in New Mexico, near Roswell. During the years after he moved to New Mexico, a thriving community of rocketry enthusiasts in the United States - the American Rocket Society - formed, drawing the attention of Navy officials. In 1942, Lieutenant Fink Fischer, a Naval Aviator interested in rocket-assist for takeoffs, approached Goddard with an offer of employment for the U.S. Navy. Goddard began work in that year at the Experiment Station facility in Annapolis, across the Severn River from the Naval Academy with then-Lieutenant Robert Truax.

Robert Truax was an American Rocket Society member who graduated from the U.S. Naval Academy in 1939. In 1937, he built a small prototype liquid-fueled rocket engine in Naval Academy machine shops, and test-fired it at the Naval Experiment Station across the Severn River from the Naval Academy.[2] This work, while small in scope (Truax's rocket only produced 25 lbs of thrust) drew the attention of the Bureau of Aeronautics, who solicited his expertise in helping to "power up" the PBY-2 *Catalina*, which was underpowered at takeoff. His application of rockets to this problem came to be known as JATO.

---

[2] Ted Wilbur. *Navy Space.* Naval Aviation News. November 1970. pp. 20-21. http://www.history.navy.mil. June 2007.

B. WORLD WAR II DEVELOPMENTS

Truax and Goddard, in the course of their experiments at the Annapolis Experiment Station, developed the groundwork for the U.S. Navy's guided missile program. Work on military rocket boosters in the early 1940s devolved into applications of solid rocket boosters because of the relative ease of construction, maintenance and durability. Army Air Corps and Bureau of Ordnance efforts were along these lines. Realizing the potential of long-range missiles and the threat they represented to the Allies, Truax and Goddard shifted their efforts to the design and development of air-to-air and surface-to-air interceptor weapons. Though they met with limited success before Goddard's death in August of 1945 and the end of the war, the technical developments in liquid-fueled rockets resulted in the Navy's BuAir publishing a study by Commander Harvey Hall and Lieutenant Robert DeHaviland entitled *"Feasibility of Space Rocketry."*[3] Truax identifies this study as the first U.S. space program – the document proposed the construction, launch and operation of an earth-orbiting satellite for scientific purposes.

In contrast to the piecemeal, fragmented and under-funded U.S. rocket efforts, the German work during the late 1930s and early '40s was well funded, organized and centrally controlled by Dr. Werner Von Braun and German Army Captain Walter Dornberger. The focus of Von Braun's efforts was based on the outstanding work conducted by Dr. Goddard, and these evolutionary designs resulted in the remarkably capable V-2 rocket. Though not used in a strategically significant manner by Germany, captured V-2s became test-bed platforms for scientific and military experiments in the U.S. following the end of the war. In this way, evolutionary engineering from Goddard's initial work in 1912 -1926 timeframe found its way back to provide the groundwork for ballistic missile research, and ultimately the U.S. space program.

C. POST-WAR CUTBACKS AND COMPETITION

Competition between the Army Air Corps (U.S. Air Force as of 1947) and the Navy space programs dates as far back as the effort to recruit Goddard – in 1942, when

---

[3] Ted Wilbur. *Navy Space.* Naval Aviation News. November 1970. pp. 20-21. http://www.history.navy.mil. June 2007.

Lieutenant Fischer approached Goddard with an employment offer, he was simultaneously being courted by the Army Air Corps to join their rocket/aviation development program.[4] Though generally genteel, the competition among the military services, and later NASA, had multiple effects. Specialization and focus on specific systems was one. Where Army and Air Force space systems design were initially focused on dominance of the strategic space environment, Navy efforts ultimately evolved towards development and utilization of space-based systems to support terrestrial operations. Early Army Ballistic Missile Agency work under Werner Von Braun (following the end of WWII, Von Braun worked for the U.S. Army) had the lofty goal of developing manned space stations, but eventually devolved to a counter-battery / anti-ballistic missile mission. The Air Force, even in these early years was focused primarily on providing force-enabling technologies to bolster their control of the "vertical dimension" and strategic bombing missions.

Struggles for programmatic control and resources were another result of the inter-service and inter-agency competition. In 1946, when the Navy introduced a proposal to perform joint development of a system that could orbit a satellite, called the *High Altitude Test Vehicle*,[5] the Army Air Force and RAND Corporation stalled negotiations while rapidly composing a 'newer' proposal on the same topic to gain control of the proposal with a 'more current' study. To its credit, this particular RAND document, *"Preliminary Design of an Experimental World-Circling Spaceship"* proved to be a seminal document, offering predictions regarding the importance of scientific instruments on orbital spacecraft and the public impact of national efforts to put men in space. Additionally, the RAND report provided ammunition to the Air Staff of the Army that "…Army Air Forces should have primary responsibility for any military satellite vehicle, considering such activity to be essentially an extension of strategic air power." This statement set the stage for the next sixty years worth of competition between the Navy and the Air Force in the arena of strategic force application and the roles and responsibilities of the services.

---

[4] Ted Wilbur. *Navy Space.* Naval Aviation News. November 1970. p. 32. http://www.history.navy.mil. June 2007.

[5] Ibid., p. 34.

The late 1940s and early 1950s were characterized by sharply reduced defense budgets, the creation of the Air Force and Department of Defense under the National Defense Act of 1947 and an attempt to reduce commitments on the part of all of the military services. 1948, in particular, was a difficult year for Navy space efforts –

> After serious exploration of concepts for putting a satellite in orbit, the Navy's committee for evaluating space rocketry folded in early 1948…, …the Navy proposed to undertake a joint project with the Air force to develop earth-orbiting satellites, a proposal that was rejected by the Air Force. Proposals for space-related activity continued to be developed by the Navy, Army and Air Force, but all such proposals were opposed by Dr. Vannevar Bush, head of the powerful joint Research and Development Board.[6] …In 1948, the Secretary of Defense reported, with respect to space: The Committee on guided Missiles recommended that efforts in the field (of earth satellite vehicles) be limited to *studies*. [7]

Inter-service rivalries, particularly between the Air Force and the Navy developed during this time as the Air Force sought to define its mission and establish hegemony within its perceived sphere of influence, while protecting its programs from the effects of drastically reduced budgets. In 1947 alone, the service-wide missile budget was reduced from $29 million to $13 million, killing 20 of 28 missile programs.[8] While the Army and Navy regrouped and consolidated their efforts in traditional mission areas, the Air Force suffered the elimination of their only ballistic missile program and was in the process of standing up Strategic Air Command and developing a concept of operations for long-range nuclear strike and defense/deterrence against the Soviet Union.[9] Finally, as part of the Air Force's efforts to define itself and identify its missions, in 1948 General

---

[6] Eddie Mitchell. *Apogee, Perigee, and Recovery: Chronology of Army Exploitation of Space.* A Rand Note. 1991. p. 13.

"In December 1945, Dr. Bush testified that it would be impossible for many years to develop a 3000-mile high-angle rocket. Dr. Bush, through the 1940s, maintained that the military was unable to provide an acceptable argument which would convince him that missiles or satellites could cost-effectively accomplish any warfighting requirement better than available aircraft or other ground systems."

[7] Gary Federici. *From the Sea to the Stars.* Naval Historical Center. July 2003. Section 1.2. http://www.history.navy.mil/books/space/index.htm. May 2007. Emphasis appears in original publication.

[8] Eddie Mitchell. *Apogee, Perigee, and Recovery: Chronology of Army Exploitation of Space.* A Rand Note. 1991. p. 14.

[9] Air Force Historical Studies Office. *Emergence of the Strategic Air Command.* https://www.airforcehistory.hq.af.mil/PopTopics/SAC.htm. June 2007.

Vandenberg, Chief of Staff of the Air Force, issued a policy statement that established satellite and space systems as an extension of strategic air power and extending that logic to place U.S. space operations under the umbrella of the Air Force.[10]

D. THE SOVIET THREAT AND MILITARY PROGRAM RESURGENCE

A return to active space systems development in the 1950s was the result of Dr. Von Braun's "...aggressive lobbying of the U.S. government to develop a satellite launch vehicle using components available from the Army Ordnance Corps."[11] This project, initially called *Orbiter,* evolved into the *Explorer 1* system - the first U.S. satellite on orbit. *Orbiter* was intended by the Army to be a tri-service project from the beginning, but the Air Force "declined to participate."[12] The national competition to be first to orbit a satellite came to a head in 1955 when President Eisenhower announced that the U.S. would "launch small, unmanned, earth orbiting satellites."[13] This proclamation came as an acknowledgement of the U.S. efforts towards the planned celebration of the International Geophysical Year (1957-1958). Additionally, Eisenhower intended the IGY project to be separate from the existing space systems under development by the armed forces. Unfortunately, no depth of experience or engineering expertise in space systems existed outside the Department of Defense, so a compromise was reached that provided for personnel from the Army and Navy to design and field a new rocket and satellite separate from the military systems under development.

The Naval Research Laboratory (NRL) floated a proposal, called *Vanguard* to launch an NRL-developed payload on a booster stack comprised of a modified *Viking* sounding rocket,[14] an *Aerobee*-derived second stage, and a newly designed third stage. *Vanguard* was in competition with a wholly Air Force program, Project *World Series,*

---

[10] Paul B. Stares. *The Militarization of Space, U.S. Policy 1945-1948*. 1985 p. 27.

[11] Gary Federici. *From the Sea to the Stars*. Naval Historical Center. July 2003. Section 1.4. http://www.history.navy.mil/books/space/index.htm. May 2007.

[12] Ibid., Section 1.4.

[13] Ted Wilbur. *Navy Space*. Naval Aviation News. November 1970. p. 34. http://www.history.navy.mil. June 2007.

[14] The Viking rockets were Naval Research Laboratory research rockets based heavily on technology from the German V-2, which in-turn, traces its lineage back to Dr. Goddard's designs.

based on the *Atlas/Aerobee* boosters and an Army program, Project *Orbiter/Explorer 1,* that used evolutionary models of the very successful *Redstone* rocket. Because the Navy's program was perceived as a "science and research" rocket system, it was chosen over the ballistic missile programs of the other services. The *Vanguard* system, with three stages, gimbaled motors, and improved fuel pumps, represented a technological leap and deviation from the established rockets and consequently was higher risk than either the Army or Air Force proposals.[15] Additionally, while the Navy had the expertise to design the satellite, and the *Viking* (first stage) was a proven system, the program had no launch pad – Army launch facilities at the Redstone Arsenal in Alabama were occupied with the Army's ballistic missile program, Jupiter, and the Navy's test range at Point Mugu, California was geared for cruise-missile tests, rather than the big orbital booster systems. Ultimately, space and money was found to construct a dedicated pad at Cape Canaveral for *Vanguard* at the Air Force's launch complex.

While the Naval Research Laboratory tried to field *Vanguard*, the Soviet Union managed to launch Sputnik aboard an SS-6 *Sapwood*, a powerful, strictly military ICBM booster on 4 October 1957. Validating the RAND report "*Preliminary Design of and Experimental World-Circling Spaceship*" negative American public reaction to the Soviet success was directed against the *Vanguard* project, which because of the array of unproven technologies involved, was well behind the Soviet schedule. President Eisenhower responded to the Sputnik launch by establishing the Advanced Research Projects Agency (ARPA, the predecessor to DARPA), and NASA in late 1957 and 1958.

E. NASA, ARPA, AND THE MILITARY BRAIN DRAIN

ARPA was created to act as the single-point for funding and development of weapons systems on the military side, and NASA was intended to be the owner of development of space systems "except…activities primarily associated with the development of weapons systems…"[16] Intended to accelerate both the civilian and

---

[15] Air University Space Primer. Chapter 1. Space History. 2003. http://space.au.af.mil/primer/. June 2007.

[16] United States. National Aeronautics and Space Act of 1958.

military development of U.S. space capabilities, the creation of these two entities further exacerbated the already competitive environment among Army, Air Force and Navy space experts. ARPA's 1957 charter under the Eisenhower administration severely restricted the Department of Defense's activities in space systems development, and worse, poisoned the research environment between Department of Defense scientists, individual service technology development centers and NASA. Additionally, despite the existence of viable space programs within all three services, ARPA awarded more than 80% of available funding to the Air Force.[17] As a consequence, in 1959, following the creation of NASA (1958), ARPA was relieved of its space projects research in 1959, and left to conduct only advanced science and technology research.

The establishment of NASA was a further disruptive occasion for the military space efforts. In 1958, the Navy transferred 300 scientists and technical personnel from the Naval Research Laboratory, and in 1960, the *Vanguard* program, with approximately 200 personnel moved from NRL ownership to NASA Goddard, in Maryland.[18] Similarly, the Army suffered a "brain-drain" with the stand-up of NASA, when in 1960 the Army transferred Dr. Werner Von Braun and the entire Army Ballistic Missile Agency Development Operations Division to NASA – including more than 150 of Von Braun's engineers, 3900 support personnel and 2500 missile and satellite technicians. This transfer came on the heels of the re-designation of the Army's Redstone Arsenal space development facility to NASA Marshall in 1958, as well as transfer of the *Redstone* and *Saturn* missile projects. With the founding of NASA and ARPA, the age of independent military service development of space systems came to an end. The centralization of funding under ARPA, the nascent bureaucracy of NASA, and the transfer of so much institutional expertise from the military services to NASA resulted in a watering-down of the culture that identified the individual military service efforts as unique.

---

[17] Joshua Boehm and Craig Baker. *A History of United States National Security Space Management and Organization*. January 2001. Section IIB. http://www.fas.org/spp/eprint/article03.html. June 2007.

[18] Gary Federici. *From the Sea to the Stars*. Naval Historical Center. July 2003. Section 1.5.1. http://www.history.navy.mil/books/space/index.htm. May 2007.

F. MILITARY PROGRAMS PRIOR TO 1961

Vanguard, finishing development amidst the pressures of Soviet competition, negative public opinion, inter-service rivalry and the challenge of NASA's standup, was a failure. The first two full-scale launches of the system with a payload exploded on the launch pad, and 60 seconds into flight, respectively. The third launch was successful, but by this point, the Secretary of Defense had ordered the Army and Werner Von Braun to prepare their *Explorer* program to launch atop a *Jupiter-C* ICBM. *Explorer 1* achieved orbit on 31 January, 1958. In the meantime, a total of eleven launches of the *Vanguard* program were attempted, only two of which were successful.

Following the two-year spasm of effort that comprised the *Vanguard* program, government investment and research in space scaled up dramatically. As the money began to flow in, the individual services were able to diversify and de-conflict their efforts in utilizing the capabilities enabled by space development. Army and Air Force efforts were split with the Army holding responsibility for development of missiles with ranges of 200 miles or less and the Air Force was given the mission of developing missiles with ranges of 200 miles or more. Additionally, the Air Force had begun work under a 1954 Office of the Secretary of Defense (OSD) charter to develop a capability to "provide surveillance of 'pre-selected areas of the earth' (read: USSR) in order to determine the status of a potential enemy's war making capability."[19] The shorter-range Army mission led to the development of the *Nike* series of continental defense surface-to-air missiles and Army Signal Corps R&D efforts resulted in prototype solar-power cells, TV broadcasts from space, space-based radio transceivers, and ground-based phased-array radar systems.[20]

The Navy, meanwhile, set to developing navigational systems to support its blue-water fleet in the escalating competition with Soviet forces and submarine-launched ballistic missile systems to ensure a role in strategic warfare. A 1954 report to the

---

[19] Gary Federici. *From the Sea to the Stars*. Naval Historical Center. July 2003. Section 1.5.4.1. http://www.history.navy.mil/books/space/index.htm. May 2007.

[20] Eddie Mitchell. *Apogee, Perigee, and Recovery: Chronology of Army Exploitation of Space*. A Rand Note. 1991. pp. 26-28.

Department of Defense chaired by MIT President, Dr. James Killian, recommended both the development of, and division of labor for, a ballistic missile force to counter the Soviet threat. This report led to Air Force development of ICBMs (Intercontinental Ballistic Missile, 5000+ mile range), Army development of IRBMs (Intermediate Range Ballistic Missile, 1500 mile range) and a joint Navy/Army program to develop the Fleet Ballistic Missile (*Polaris*), a derivative of the IRBM. The joint program leveraged the Army's experience in booster development, and levied the requirement on the Navy to develop the sea-based launching system. Initially beneficial for both the Army and Navy, the program provided the Army with a requirement to defend against Air Force encroachment, and the Navy a method to get into the strategic weapons business. Eventually, the partnership was dissolved by Navy development of solid fuels that were denser and more compact than the Army *Jupiter* propellant that powered the initial *Polaris* missiles. The *Polaris* program was spearheaded by Captain Robert Freitag, an MIT-trained engineer and salesman par-excellence, along with Captain Robert Truax. Freitag and Truax, during the process of promoting the *Polaris* program, came to realize that the new missile system, in combination with other navy space programs like *Transit* (navigation) and *Courier* (communication), was about to change some of the fundamental practices of the entire Navy.[21] They assisted in convening a cross-disciplinary board in 1959 that established two space sections under OPNAV to better centralize policy and activity in Navy space development.

The *Transit* satellite navigation system was a result of a surfeit of intellectual curiosity on the part of a pair of Johns Hopkins Applied Physics Laboratory personnel in 1957. APL researchers William Guier and George Wieffenbach, fascinated by the launch of *Sputnik I,* discovered that they could accurately track the satellite by processing Doppler shift data.[22] With this capability, APL scientists realized that they could provide precise positional data for earth-bound navigation based on satellites with known position, timing data and Doppler information from a broadcast signal. This APL

---

[21] Ted Wilbur. *Navy Space.* Naval Aviation News. November 1970. pp. 56-59. http://www.history.navy.mil. June 2007.

[22] Gary Federici. *From the Sea to the Stars.* Naval Historical Center. July 2003. Section 1.6.1. http://www.history.navy.mil/books/space/index.htm. May 2007.

concept was sponsored by the Navy in 1958, and proposed for development as the *Transit* system. *Transit* was a groundbreaking development in that it was the first space system to be fielded as a method of addressing a specifically terrestrial problem. As a predecessor to the Air Force's NAVSTAR GPS system (contracted in 1974), 26 *Transit* satellites were launched between September of 1959 and October 1977. This system evolved to support approximately 25-meter accuracy, but the wait time to get enough satellite passes to resolve position sometimes took minutes, making it unsuitable for fast moving receivers, like aircraft. Requirements generated from *Transit* eventually found their way to the GPS program, helping refine Navy needs during the Air Force requirements definition process.

G. FIRST ESTABLISHMENT OF THE "EXECUTIVE AGENT FOR SPACE"

By 1961, the modern scheme of military satellite launch and operation had begun to emerge. Secretary of Defense Robert McNamara signed Defense Directive 5160.32 in March of 1961, assigning the Air Force sole responsibility for development and acquisition of all U.S. military space systems. The other services were permitted to perform research in space systems and technology, but were not allowed to field in-house developed systems. Driven by a January 1961 report[23] headed up by Dr. Jerome Wiesner of MIT (later, President Emeritus of MIT) that attributed the Soviet lead in space to lack of coordination and duplicated efforts by the U.S. military establishment, the Secretary of the Air Force lobbied the Office of the Secretary of Defense for the lead role in managing U.S. military space systems development. Award of this mission to the Air Force resulted in the establishment of the Air Force Systems Command and appointment of the Secretary of the Air Force as the Department of Defense Executive Agent for Space. This appointment came as a surprise to the other services. The Navy, in particular, already had congressional approval for its 1962 – 1965 space program budget and was in development and fielding of the *Transit* navigational system.[24]

---

[23] Wiesner Committee,"Report to the President-Elect of the Ad Hoc Committee on Space." NASA History Office. 10 January 1961. http://www.hq.nasa.gov/office/pao/History/report61.html. June 2007.

[24] Gary Federici. *From the Sea to the Stars*. Naval Historical Center. July 2003. Section 2.1.2. http://www.history.navy.mil/books/space/index.htm. May 2007.

The 1961 Department of Defense Directive 5160.32 resulted in a decade-long slowdown in military space development as NASA budgets and manned space flight efforts took center stage in the space arena, and the Vietnam War absorbed budgets that the services had otherwise used for research and development. Nonetheless, science and technology development, outside the purview of the Air Force's Executive Agent status, continued in both the Army and Navy.

The Army established the Strategic Communications Command, in 1964 to manage continuing Army R&D on the Defense Satellite Communication System (*DSCS*).[25] *DSCS* is a protected, high-bandwidth satellite communications system developed by the Army, but procured, launched and operated by the Air Force. Originally a near-geosynchronous drifting satellite, twenty-six *DSCS I* satellites were launched by the Air Force between 1966 and 1968 to provide long-haul, high-bandwidth communications pipes to large, stationary Army forces. *DSCS* in its present form, *DSCS III* and *DSCS III SLEP* (Service Life Extension Program), provides worldwide high data rate communications in the Super High Frequency (SHF) band for stationary and mobile platforms capable of mounting a four- to seven-foot antenna. *DSCS III* satellites, launched from 1982 and later, are geosynchronous and are capable of communicating in protected and jam resistant modes. *DSCS* is exceptionally important to the Navy, and provides the sole full-duplex, military high-bandwidth communication link to large-deck ships.

Likewise, Navy science and technology development continued through the 1960s in the face of increasing Air Force domination of the space arena. Navy experimentation in the fields of space surveillance (VHF Fence), ionospheric research (NASA *Explorer*), VLF communication (*LOFTI*), electronic intelligence (*SURCAL*) and space weather and solar observation (*SOLRAD*) continued through the decade.[26] Additionally, engineering development on specialized satellite control systems and upper-stage technologies was

---

[25] Joshua Boehm and Craig Baker. *A History of United States National Security Space Management and Organization.* January 2001. Section IIIA. http://www.fas.org/spp/eprint/article03.html. June 2007.

[26] Gary Federici. *From the Sea to the Stars.* Naval Historical Center. July 2003. Various. http://www.history.navy.mil/books/space/index.htm. May 2007.

conducted by the Naval Research Laboratory. NRL scientists developed gravity gradient stabilization techniques that were fielded aboard a *Transit* satellite in 1963, powerful cold-gas thrusters for stationkeeping that were launched on *SOLRAD* in 1965, and multiple-payload launches were pioneered with NRL assistance throughout the 1960s. Finally, the *Transit* navigation system, first launched in September 1959, was the most successful of the Navy science projects. *Transit* technology, and the expertise acquired during its development became instrumental in the development of the NAVSTAR GPS system, and refinement of requirements for the GPS constellation to support the Navy user.[27]

H. SPACE PROGRAM DIVERGENCE IN THE MILITARY SERVICES

By 1970, a joint Army-Navy lobbying effort to overturn the 1961 DoD Directive was successful, allowing those services to return to active development of "specialized satellite systems for ocean surveillance, communication, navigation, meteorology, mapping, charting and geodesy."[28] The new 1970 DoD Directive 5160.32 permitted a great expansion of the Navy space effort, and led directly to the development of technologies enabling the current concepts of "FORCEnet"[29] and "information superiority" – *FLTSAT*, UHF Follow-On (*UFO*), *GEOSAT*, and shipboard terminals supporting communication with the *DSCS* constellation.

It was during this time, in the mid-1970s when Navy relations with Air Force program offices and program management fell to unprecedented lows. The *FLTSAT* program, in particular, was plagued with problems between the specifications and requirements organization, the NRL, and the contracting organization, USAF Space and Missiles Systems Organization. Air Force management practices were seemingly incompatible with Naval Research Lab organizational culture, and when technical difficulties arose in the construction and testing of the satellites, the Air Force's

---

[27] Gary Federici. *From the Sea to the Stars*. Naval Historical Center. July 2003. Section 3.4.3. http://www.history.navy.mil/books/space/index.htm. May 2007.

[28] United States. Department of Defense Directive 5160.32, March 1961.

[29] Department of the Navy. http://forcenet.navy.mil/. June 2007.

Aerospace Corporation, brought in to resolve the problems, initially sought a solution by questioning the NRL base specifications for the satellite.[30] Though exceptional compromise and cross-cultural team-building among a coterie of dedicated Navy and Air Force officers saved the program, this clash of organizational cultures was indicative of the forming institutional mentalities in the military space arena

Resurgence in space capabilities and technological innovation leading to the modern era is traced by multiple authors[31] to the late 1970s, with the inception of the TENCAP (Tactical Exploitation of National Capabilities) program among all three services. TENCAP was executed differently among the services, but generally, TENCAP efforts have been focused on high-technology efforts leveraging the capabilities of National systems to support tactical warfighting. Navy TENCAP efforts trend towards scientific research and development, with less emphasis on acquisition and lifecycle of systems. This "leveraging" of space systems and other service capabilities has become a hallmark of naval space applications in general, reducing the Navy's required service-specific investment in space while achieving the necessary capabilities to provide support to the fleet.

I. **ESTABLISHMENT OF THE UNITED STATES SPACE COMMAND AND GROWTH OF NAVAL SPACE**

Growing reliance on space as a medium to support terrestrial naval operations began to meet with high-level recognition in the Navy in the early 1980s, and in 1983, the Secretary of the Navy stood up Naval Space Command to centralize control of naval space efforts. The founding of the Naval Space Command came at a time when increased attention by Congress on the progress and organization of U.S. space efforts was reaching a fever pitch. The Air Force was an early victim of the congressional attention in the 1980s, with the U.S. Senate Subcommittee on Strategic and Theater Nuclear Programs pushing for organizational efficiencies in the strategic combat arena, and Resolution 5130 being introduced in the House of Representatives by Congressman Ken Kramer (R, CO)

---

[30] Gary Federici. *From the Sea to the Stars*. Naval Historical Center. July 2003. Section 3.3.4.2. http://www.history.navy.mil/books/space/index.htm. May 2007.

[31] Various: See Federici, Mitchell and Boehm.

to rename the Air Force to the "Aerospace Force."[32] Finally, a Government Accountability Office (GAO) report issued in January of 1982 was typically critical of the Department of Defense's management of space capabilities, and recommended reorganization and consolidation of the various DoD space functions at the Consolidated Space Operations Center in Colorado Springs.[33] Shortly thereafter, in September of 1982, the Air Force founded the Air Force Space Command.

The existence of consolidated Air Force and Navy Space Commands provided sufficient impetus for the creation of a joint service space command, and in September of 1985, the Joint Chiefs of Staff created the United States Space Command. Interestingly, U.S. Space Command came into existence in-part because of the institutional inertia developed during the early 1980s to centralize control of military space efforts, and also because of the extensive R&D being conducted for the Strategic Defense Initiative, President Ronald Reagan's space-based weapons system for anti-ballistic weapons defense. Doctrinal and policy developments that preceded the standup of USSPACECOM came in July of 1984, when the National Security Council conducted a review and update of the national space strategy. Immediately following, in August of 1984, the National Space Strategy National Security Decision Directive was released, paving the way for the establishment of U.S. Space Command.

Meanwhile, the Army, which was in the midst of a baseline review of its fighting doctrine, was working to incorporate requirements for persistent overhead surveillance, beyond line-of-sight-communications and maneuver warfare.[34] This doctrine, AirLand Battle (FM 100-5) relied extremely heavily on space systems infrastructure, and in

---

[32] Joshua Boehm and Craig Baker. *A History of United States National Security Space Management and Organization.* January 2001. Section IIIA. http://www.fas.org/spp/eprint/article03.html. June 2007.

The terms "Aerospace" and "Aerospace force" remains a sensitive topic within the Air Force. See "The Transformation Trinity" by Major Bruce H. McClintock, USAF (Air University thesis).

[33] Joshua Boehm and Craig Baker. *A History of United States National Security Space Management and Organization.* January 2001. Section IIIA. http://www.fas.org/spp/eprint/article03.html. June 2007.

[34] Eddie Mitchell. *Apogee, Perigee, and Recovery: Chronology of Army Exploitation of Space.* A Rand Note. 1991. pp. 73-77.

The Army's new doctrine of combat, developed from 1978 to 1982, was termed AirLand Battle. It postulated operations over vast areas, with weapons-dense battlefields, extremely short reaction times and scarce resupply opportunities.

recognition of that requirement, by August of 1986, the Army had established the Army Space Agency (renamed Army Space Command in April 1988) as the Army component of U.S. Space Command.

Despite the premise that the Naval Space Command (NAVSPACECOM) was to be the central point for Navy space effort, it did not function as the sole Navy entity in the arena. NAVSPACECOM was instead the operational commander of a trio of organizations:

- Navy Space Systems Division (OP-943) whose mission it was to validate and sponsor programs.
- NAVELEXSYSCOM (PME-106) which executed contract programs and delivered space systems.
- NAVSPACECOM to collect and validate requirements for satellite support of fleet operations.[35]

Naval Space Command became a clearing-house for other Navy space-related organizations and the mission of training and educating Naval leadership. Missions and subordinate commands up until its disestablishment in 2002 included:

- Navy Astronautics Group (renamed Naval Satellite Operation Center in 1990)
- Naval Space Surveillance Center (capabilities turned over to the Air Force in 2003)[36]
- Fleet Surveillance Support Command
- Naval Space Command Reserve Units
- Marine Corps Reserve Augmentation Unit
- Naval Space Command Detachment, Colorado Springs (USSPACECOM Liaison)
- Naval Space Command Detachment ECHO (DSP/JTAGS)
- Navy TENCAP
- Alternate Space Defense Operations Center (merged with Alternate Space Surveillance Center to create Alternate Space Control Center)

---

[35] Gary Federici. *From the Sea to the Stars*. Naval Historical Center. July 2003. Section 4.10.2. http://www.history.navy.mil/books/space/index.htm. May 2007.

[36] Gary R. Wagner. *Navy Transfers Space Surveillance Mission to the Air Force.* Navy Newstand. 20 October 2004. http://www.news.navy.mil/search/display.asp?story_id=15597. June 2007.

By the 1990s, the Naval Space Command had become an organization entrusted with a wide variety of combat support mission areas of critical importance to the fleet. The Naval Satellite Operations Center, for instance, though comprised of only approximately 150 personnel, was responsible for UHF communications for the 1990-1991 Desert Shield/Desert Storm operations. UHF communications, on *FLTSAT* and UHF Follow-On (*UFO*) satellites, comprised the only 'tactical' overhead communications service for ground forces at that time. Additionally, Navy TENCAP, working with the Army, pushed for greater capabilities realization of the Defense Support Program assets (DSP was initially designed to sense ballistic missile launch in the Cold War era), and developed a system called JTAGS to monitor theater missile launch (SCUD) in the Desert Storm Area of Operations.

J. THE CONTESTED MISSION AREA AND NATIONAL SPACE REORGANIZATION

Navy space operations in the same vein as the DSP/JTAGS effort have met with stiff and growing resistance from the Air Force and their partners in the Intelligence Community. As U.S. national space capabilities matured towards the end of the 20th century, the organizations that developed the greatest capability, acquired the largest budgets and established the most lengthy personnel rosters began to approach space as if it were their exclusive provenance. This proprietary attitude hearkens back to the 1961 DoD Directive naming the Air Force as the Executive Agent for Space and the 1960 founding of the National Reconnaissance Office (NRO). Notwithstanding the cancellation of this directive in 1970, as space budgets and programs migrated to these two organizations beginning in the 1960s, they forged an institutional mentality that much as the Navy 'ownership' of the seas was uncontested by the other services, the Air

Force should 'own' the "vertical dimension."[37] A Time Magazine article from March 17th of 1961 details the implications clearly:

> Aerospace Force?
>
> The U.S. Air Force has been trying the name "U.S. Aerospace Force" on its tongue ever since the Eisenhower Administration assigned it prime responsibility for "space transportation." Last week the name sounded better than ever when Defense Secretary Robert McNamara, over the strangled cries of other services, flatly assigned "space development programs and projects to the Department of the Air Force except under unusual circumstances."
>
> No existing programs were changed. The Army will continue with its Advent communications satellite; the Navy will stick with its Transit navigation satellite. And each service, in Pentagon parlance, will have "the right to think," to do research on the problems of putting its weapons into space. But from now on, the Air Force is boss of the big boosters that make military space ventures possible.
>
> Despite this truce, there are still new galaxies to conquer before the Aerospace Force becomes the big cheese. There is still an ill-defined line between military projects and work done by the civilian National Aeronautics and Space Administration. Some day soon, the President will have to set up a single, economical space agency. Airmen are betting that it will belong to them.[38]

Regardless of the fact that this article was written more than 45 years ago, it clearly summarizes an aim of the modern-day Air Force – exertion of organizational control over the air and space environments. The specific "Aerospace" concept, however, has recently fallen into disfavor. Since the later 1990s, semantic and organizational issues regarding the use of the "Aerospace" have been raised by Air Force officers as a dilution of the service's primary mission of air superiority. This has resulted

---

[37] F.W. Peters & Michael E. Ryan. *The Aerospace Force: Defending America in the 21st Century…a White Paper on Aerospace Integration.* Department of the Air Force, Washington D.C. 2000. http://stinet.dtic.mil/cgi-bin/GetTRDoc?AD=ADA381077&Location=U2&doc=GetTRDoc.pdf. June 2007. The term "vertical dimension" occurs no fewer than four times in this particular document, and appears in almost every scholarly paper on or by the Air Force that the authors have reviewed. The origin of the term, which is used to imply a volume without bound, starting at the Earth's surface, seems to come from the same timeframe as the 1961 DoD Directive 5160.32 appointing the Air Force as the Executive Agent for Space.

[38] Time Magazine. *Aerospace Force?* 17 March 1961. http://www.time.com/time/magazine/article/0,9171,894428,00.html. June 2007.

in funding battles between the air-breathing programs and the development and fielding of orbital and launch systems. Current discussion and doctrine leans towards the identification of "Space-specific" forces, and the establishment of a "Space Warfighting" community or U.S. Space Force.[39]

In the face of increasing Air Force space budgets, restrictions on service exploitation of the space arena and ambivalence from leadership, Navy space efforts are under-represented in comparison with the relative importance of space effects and space support to the fleet. The mid-1990s represented the pinnacle of the modern Navy space organization.[40] During these years, in the aftermath of Desert Storm, leadership and "warfighter" recognition of the Navy's reliance on robust satellite systems for command, control, communications and intelligence (C^3I) functions reached its peak. Development of accurate, guided munitions, complex operations plans transmitted via computer networks, Intelligence Preparation of the Battlespace and expectations of instantaneous, pervasive, worldwide communications reinforced the understanding of senior leaders of the necessity for space-borne capabilities and expertise. Unfortunately, sometime between the late 1990s and the present day this understanding disappeared.

A possible source for the second decline in Navy space involvement may stem from the reorganization of Department of Defense space management during the Clinton Administration. Fiscal year 1993 and 1994 Defense Authorization and Defense Appropriations Bills respectively mandated centralized space acquisition for the reduction of costs, and stated that then-current management structures within DoD space were inadequate.[41] In response, the position of Deputy Undersecretary of Defense for Space (DUSD Space) was created to "…serve as the principal point of contact within

---

[39] See McClintock and Harter.

[40] Joshua Boehm and Craig Baker. *A History of United States National Security Space Management and Organization.* January 2001. Section IIIB2. http://www.fas.org/spp/eprint/article03.html. June 2007.
Following the merger of NAVSPACECOM with the Naval Space Surveillance Center, consolidated operations in Navy space included elements exercising control of operational management of space systems, operation of the Naval Space Surveillance Network, operational and tactical support to Naval forces and status as the Alternate Space Control Center for the U.S. Space Command. Not since this time have all of these functions been consolidated under one command.

[41] United States. *National Space issues: Observation on Defense Space Program and Activities.* Government Accountability Office. 16 August 1994. GAO/NSIAD-94-253, 10.

OSD for space matters, to develop, coordinate, and oversee implementation of DoD space policy and to provide oversight over all DoD Space architectures and the acquisition of DoD space programs."[42] Rapid organizational changes followed:

- 1995, March – DoD Space Architect established. "This office was established to consolidate the responsibilities for DoD space missions and system architecture development, to eliminate "stovepiped" space programs, and to improve efficiencies in acquisition and future operations in support of U.S. military operations."[43] The DoD SA, an Air Force two-star, worked "with" the Deputy Undersecretary of Defense for Space.

- 1995, December – Joint Space Management Board (JSMB) established. Created jointly by the Secretary of Defense and Director of the CIA to "consolidate defense and intelligence space architecture functions into a single national space architecture."[44]

- 1997, January – Defense Reform Initiatives 11 and 42 announced. Intended to "streamline" DoD organization and infrastructure through the use of business practices, these two initiatives resulted in yet another DoD Space restructuring.

- 1998, July – DoD Space Architect renamed National Security Space Architect. Job description of DoD SA broadened to include incorporation of Intelligence Community assets and architectures into the DoD Space architecture.

- 2001 – Space Commission releases report critical of DoD management of space organization and capabilities.

- 2003, June – In an echo of the 1961 DoD Directive 5160.32, the U.S. Air Force is identified as the Executive Agent for Space in response to the 2001 Space Commission report. (DoD Directive 5101.2)

The result of this gusty and shifting organizational climate seems to have resulted in disinterest and indifference on the part of senior Navy leadership. On 11 July 2002, the Naval Space Command was disestablished and Naval Network Warfare Command (NETWARCOM) was established. This new organization encompassed and superseded the strictly space-focused organization, incorporating space capabilities (primarily in the communications realm) as a portion of an overarching mission to provide networked

---

[42] Joshua Boehm and Craig Baker. *A History of United States National Security Space Management and Organization.* January 2001. Section IIE1. http://www.fas.org/spp/eprint/article03.html. June 2007.

[43] Joshua Boehm and Craig Baker. *A History of United States National Security Space Management and Organization.* January 2001. Section IIF2. http://www.fas.org/spp/eprint/article03.html. June 2007.

[44] Ibid., Section IIF3.

communications and resources to the Navy. Incorporation of the Naval Space Command into the NETWARCOM mission relegated the space mission area to a secondary and supporting status within the enterprise's task hierarchy, and ultimately contributed to the incipient and crippling loss of direction in the Navy space community.

When they were absorbed into NETWARCOM, the Naval Space Command numbered approximately 400 personnel. At that time, the Air Force Space Command numbered approximately 33,600,[45] and was charged with the lion's share of the Department of Defense space budget. Air Force-provided numbers for the space community, in the year 2000 read as shown in Table 1, below:

Space Personnel	90%
Space Budget	85%
Space Assets	86%
Space Infrastructure	90%

Table 1. Air Force Percentage of DoD Space Capabilities.[46]

While critically reliant on space systems to perform its terrestrial mission, the Navy has seen fit to pursue a policy of leveraging the capabilities provided by other organizations to achieve its combat requirements. Unfortunately, quality-of-service concerns in many facets of the National Security Space mission areas,[47] relating to both USAF- and Intelligence Community-provided resources have plagued this relationship.

---

[45] Bruce H. McClintock, Major, U.S. Air Force. *The Transformation Trinity.* Air University Press, Maxwell AFB, Alabama. 2002. p.42.

[46] F.W. Peters & Michael E. Ryan. *The Aerospace Force: Defending America in the 21st Century...a White Paper on Aerospace Integration.* Department of the Air Force, Washington D.C. 2000. p. 5. http://stinet.dtic.mil/cgi-bin/GetTRDoc?AD=ADA381077&Location=U2&doc=GetTRDoc.pdf. June 2007.

[47] The authors and editors of *The Navy's Needs in Space for Providing Future Capabilities* identify the following six mission areas – ISR, METOC, TBMD, Communications, PNT, and Space Control, while the National Security Space Office identifies a larger, more granular group of missions including – Surveillance and Warning, MilSatCom, Navigation, Environmental Monitoring, ISR, Space Surveillance, NMD/Counterspace, Space Forces Support, Force Application, General Support and Technology RDT&E. http://www.wslfweb.org/docs/roadmap/irm/rmindex.htm. June 2007.

Incompatible mindsets between space-resource operators - who in many cases viewed their mission as an end-unto-itself - and the operational user of space-sourced functionality led to dissatisfaction on the part of the end user, and a perception on the part of the space systems operator that their resources were being misused. Fortunately, restructuring initiatives in the late 1990s, resulting from DoD and congressional concerns about space support to military forces during the 1991 Gulf War, relieved some of the friction. Although elements of this problem persist, operational space support of the terrestrial warfighter has improved dramatically since this restructuring of management of National Security Space functions in the late 1990s.[48] Most notably, mandates to "...facilitate the cross-coordination of both classified and unclassified space products..."[49] and allocation and future plans for communications resources have served to spread oil on troubled waters.

With increasing reliance on outsourcing to provide space-based capabilities and services, the Navy has demonstrated a progressively diminishing interest in the business of space in recent years. Program management of communications satellites in the UHF band reflects the last vestige of a dedicated Navy commitment to acquiring space systems, and even these programs comprise Navy involvement for primarily historical reasons. In the present day, ever-increasing reliance on high-bandwidth communications systems force the Navy to use systems acquired and operated by the Air Force and Army (*MILSTAR*, *DSCS*) or services provided by commercial vendors. Likewise, overhead surveillance, navigation, weather and science and technology needs that in the past were developed by the Navy to meet internal needs are coming from other organizations. This decline in institutional involvement in space reflects a larger struggle, as the Navy attempts to define a role for itself in an era of asymmetric warfare and largely land-based counter-insurgency operations.[50] Focus of effort and funding at the highest levels is

---

[48] United States. *Space Program Executive Overview for FY1998-2003*. Department of Defense. March 1997. http://www.fas.org/spp/military/program/sp97. June 2007.

[49] United States. *Space Program Executive Overview for FY1998-2003*. Department of Defense. March 1997. http://www.fas.org/spp/military/program/sp97. June 2007.

[50] George Galdorisi, Dr. Stephanie Hszieh and Terry McKearney. *SPAWAR Supports the Navy's Global Maritime Partnership*. CHIPS. April-June 2007. http://www.chips.navy.mil/archives/07_Jun/web_pages/Maritime_Partnership.html. June 2007.

concentrated on purchases of traditional equipment, even when the utility of $4 billion aircraft carriers and submarines becomes increasingly dependent on network-centric concepts of operations[51] and its attendant space systems.[52]

In an environment of meager budgets, minimal manpower and apparent leadership disinterest, modern-day maintenance of space capabilities has primarily been the result of dedicated individuals and isolated pockets of corporate expertise. Preservation of a full-spectrum effort in space systems development, fielding and operation no longer makes sense – the Navy focus for future space efforts should be sharpened and refined, separating unnecessary services and functions from those that best support the institution's goals and ability to perform its core warfighting responsibilities.

---

[51] David S. Alberts, John J. Garstga and Frederick P. Stein. *Network Centric Warfare: Developing and Leveraging Information Superiority.* CCRP. 2001.

[52] National Research Council. Committee on the Navy's Needs in Space for Providing Future Capabilities. *The Navy's Needs in Space for Providing Future Capabilities.* The National Academies Press 2005. Executive Summary. http://books.nap.edu/openbook.php?record_id=11200&page=1. June 2007. This document identifies Navy efforts in nine out of sixteen areas of space expertise as displaying "…little to no evidence of responsive naval management actions."

THIS PAGE INTENTIONALLY LEFT BLANK

II. SIGNIFICANT DEFINITIONS

As Department of Defense space efforts continue to evolve and transform, so do the doctrines and instructions relating to those activities. Directly connected to the DoD efforts, the United States Navy's doctrine, organizations and publications relating to space are also evolving. This chapter is intended to enhance understanding of the numerous publications, organizations and doctrines fundamental to the Navy space program in an effort to establish a baseline for further discussions in the following chapters.

This chapter is broken down into two major segments: Organizations and Concepts. The first segment essentially describes the fundamental structure of the different services and joint space organizations. The second segment focuses on the conceptual ideology and doctrine relating to the Department of Defense and specifically the Navy's space efforts.

A. ORGANIZATIONS

1. January 11, 2001 U.S. Commission to Assess National Security Space Management and Organizations (2001 Space Commission)

The 2001 Space Commission was established in 1999 by an amendment to the FY 2000 defense authorization bill. Senator Bob Smith (R-N.H.) was the point person in Congress for the creation of the Space Commission.[53] Smith believed that the annual defense budgets were continually short-changing space programs. He also noticed that military personnel without space backgrounds were being promoted faster than those with space experience and he alleged that treaties had negotiated away the U.S. advantages in space. The thirteen-member commission was chaired by Donald Rumsfeld prior to his appointment as Secretary of Defense. Among other issues, the commission sought to determine if changes needed to be made to improve the United States' national security posture and capabilities in space. Six months of research and interviews with the

---

[53] Tom Barry. *Rumsfeld Space Commission.* International Relations Center Right Web. 21 May 2004. http://rightweb.irc-online.org/profile/2820. June 2007.

25

country's leading space experts convinced the commission that space should be elevated to the status of a top national security priority. A Rumsfeld Space Commission news release called the likelihood of future conflict in space "a virtual certainty." As a result, the commission determined that the United States should take immediate steps to develop superior space capabilities.[54]

2. Naval Network Warfare Command (NETWARCOM)

Naval Network Warfare Command creates warfighting and business options for the Fleet to fight and win in the information age. They deliver and operate a reliable, secure and battle-ready global network. They lead the development, integration and execution of Information Operations effect for the Fleet. Additionally this command is charged with the mission of ensuring the Navy fully leverages and influences national space capabilities. NETWARCOM increases the naval commanders' warfighting capabilities through the use of cumulative space effects in maritime operations as measured by a maturity model.[55]

In May of 2005, the Chief of Naval Operations released the Navy Space Policy Implementation (OPNAV Instruction 5400.43) designating Commander, NETWARCOM as the Space Type Commander (TYCOM) and Space Cadre Functional Authority for the United States Navy. NETWARCOM is responsible for developing, maintaining and overseeing the Navy Space Human Capital Strategy, SSFA, PEO Space Systems and the Space Cadre Advisor. NETWARCOM is under the command of U.S. Fleet Forces Command. The U.S. Fleet Forces Command acts as the U.S. Navy functional component

---

[54] Gerry J. Gilmore. *'Space Increasingly Important,' SPACECOM Chief Says*. American Forces Press Service. 5 April 2001. http://www.defenselink.mil/news/newsarticle.aspx?id=45030. May 2007

[55] Department of the Navy. *Naval Network Warfare Command Strategic Plan 2006-2010...a framework for decision-making. Executive Summary Version 2.0*. Naval Network Warfare Command. 23 March 2007.
http://www.netwarcom.navy.mil/NETWARCOM%20Strategic%20Plan_Executive%20Version%202_1%2011.pdf. June 2007

to U.S. Strategic Command for Space.[56] NETWARCOM is tasked with standing up the NETWARCOM Maritime Operations Center (MOC) Space Cell,[57] an organization intended to provide the fleet with space effects and other space related products.

3. NETWARCOM (NNWC) Maritime Operations Center (MOC) Space Cell

Located at NETWARCOM Headquarters is the NNWC Maritime Operations Center Space Cell. The Space Cell provides NNWC with internal space situational awareness while synchronizing with the MOC IO and NETOPS (Network Operations) cells for synergistic effects. The MOC Space Cell was stood up to provide fleet forces with a single point of reach back connectivity with regards to fleet space needs and operational integration. At the operational level, the NNWC MOC Space Cell provides reach-back support to fleet MHQ/MOC Staffs, to include planning augmentation and theater level synchronization. At the tactical level, the cell provides tailored reach-back support to CSG/ESG Staffs incorporating space situational awareness reports and Space Effects Packages with a maritime domain focus. This product is low bandwidth-compatible to enable transmission and receipt in a bandwidth-challenged environment.[58]

4. Naval Satellite Operations Center (NAVSOC)

NAVSOC is responsible for operating, managing and maintaining assigned satellite systems; providing reliable satellite services for the Navy in direct support of the warfighter. NAVSOC Headquarters are in Point Mugu, California. Currently, they control the spacecraft bus for eight *UFO* (UHF Follow-On), two Polar EHF, two *FLTSAT/FEP*, one *GFO*, and four *NIMS* satellites. NAVSOC maintains operational

---

[56] Department of the Navy. OPNAVINST 5400.43A, *Navy Space Policy Implementation*. 12 February 2007. p. 9.
https://doni.daps.dla.mil/Directives/Forms/AllItems.aspx?RootFolder=%2fDirectives%2f05000%20General%20Management%20Security%20and%20Safety%20Services%2f05%2d400%20Organization%20and%20Functional%20Support%20Services. May 2007.

[57] Formerly known as the Network, Information Operations, and Space Center (NIOSC) Space Cell.

[58] Julie Niedermaier, Commander, U.S. Navy. *Navy Space Cadre Update (SSFA Space Indoctrination)*. PowerPoint Brief. March 2007.

control of these satellites from five different remote ground stations, shown in Figure 1, below, throughout the United States and Guam.

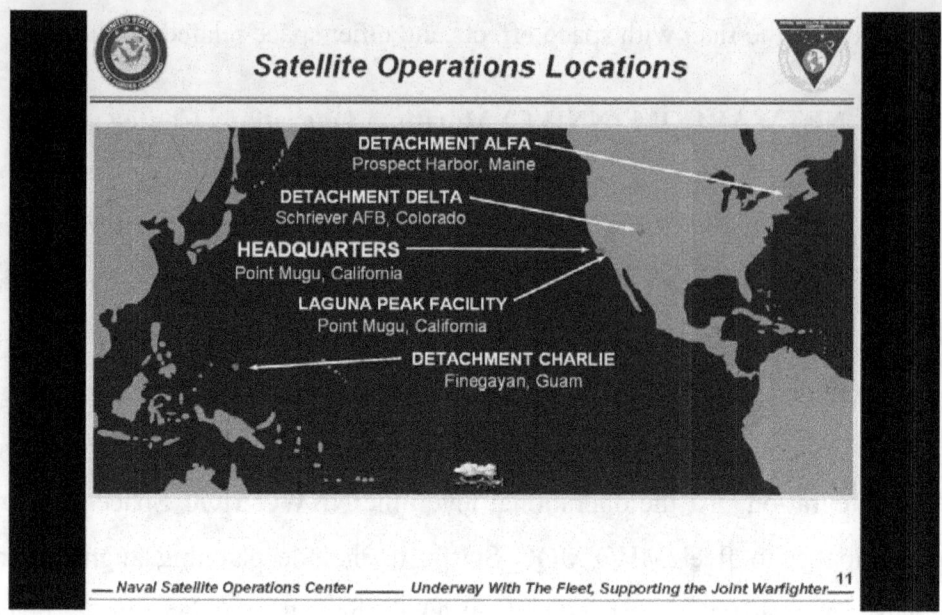

Figure 1.　NAVSOC Satellite Operations Locations[59]

Table 2, below, provides a detailed list of the functions that NAVSOC performs for each satellite under their respective control.

	HQ	LP	ALFA	CHARLIE	DELTA
FLTSAT	TT&C		TLM Collection, EHF Term Ops,	TLM Collection, EHF Term Ops	TT&C
UFO	TT&C		TLM Collection, EHF Term Ops	TLM Collection, EHF Term Ops	TT&C
POLAR	Backup T&C		Primary T&C		Host Liaison, Anomaly Resolution
GFO	T&C, Doppler Collect, Orbit Determination	Antenna Site, Backup T&C	Ant Site, Backup T&C, Doppler Collection	Doppler Collection	
NIMS	T&C				

Table 2.　NAVSOC Functional Control by Location[60]

---

[59] Paul M. Insch, Captain, U.S. Navy. *NAVSOC Command Brief*. Naval Satellite Operations Center. PowerPoint Brief. June 2006. Slide 11.

[60] Ibid., Slide 38.

In addition to the legacy systems listed above, NAVSOC is the planned controlling authority for the Mobile-User Objective System, the follow-on to the UFO systems. The orbital component of the *MUOS* system is scheduled to be operational by 2010. NAVSOC is poised to take control of the bus for five *MUOS* satellites by the year 2015.

5. Maritime Headquarters with Maritime Operations Center (MHQ-MOC)

The concept of a Maritime Headquarters with Maritime Operations Center (MHQ with MOC) evolved from Flag-level deliberations concerning the roles and capabilities of the US Navy at the operational-level of war (OLW). There is a breach between the current tactical expertise of the US Navy and enduring CCDR requirements to support theater-wide strategies and national objectives. The Navy must modify command organizations in Echelons II and III (NCCs, Numbered Fleet commanders and principal headquarters commanders) to better support operational-level planning, execution and assessment. The establishment of MHQs with MOC will support execution of the National Strategy on Maritime Security (NSMS), comply with CNO 2006 Guidance, and fulfill CCDR requirements specified in the Unified Command Plan (UCP). The Global War on Terrorism (GWOT) demands a responsive MHQ with MOC capability. It requires fully-networked naval C2 of joint operations and supporting activities incorporating the concept and capabilities of centralized guidance, distributed/collaborative planning, and decentralized execution, which synchronizes the Navy across all areas of responsibility (AOR). [61]

6. Carrier Strike Group (CSG)

The Carrier Strike Group is a flexible maritime combat-force organization construct centered on the aircraft carrier and its assigned Carrier Air Wing. The term "Carrier Strike Group" replaced the term "Carrier Battle Group" in 2003 by CNO directive. The CSG typically consists of one aircraft carrier (CVN), one *Aegis* guided missile cruiser (CG), two *Aegis* guided missile destroyers (DDG), one attack submarine (SSN) and usually one fast combat supply ship (AOE). The CSG Staff is embarked aboard the carrier and is led by a one- or two-star admiral.

---

[61] Department of the Navy. *Maritime Headquarters with Maritime Operations Center Concept of Operations (CONOPS), Final DRAFT Version.* 15 May 2006. p. ii.

7. Joint Space Operations Center (JSpOC)

The JSpOC is the operational command and control (C²) center that provides Commander, Joint Forces Component Command, Space (CDR JFCC Space), via the Commander, Joint Space Operations (CDRJSO), the capability to plan, task, direct, synchronize, and assess the activities of assigned and attached space forces (as well as those space forces made available for tasking)... CDR JFCC Space executes OPCON of space forces via the JSpOC at Vandenberg AFB, CA.[62]

The JSpOC maintains a twenty-four hour watch floor with reach-back capability for the NNWC MOC Space Cell and Navy Space Cadre. They conduct strategic planning and operational tasking for space effects across the entire DoD space spectrum. Similar to that of an Air Tasking Order (ATO), the JSpOC is responsible for the weekly publishing of a Space Tasking Order (STO) in which they assign weekly requirements for space assets throughout the globe. They are also responsible for publishing the special instructions (SIPNS) for all joint space activity.

8. Government Accountability Office (GAO)

The Government Accountability Office, the audit, evaluation and investigative arm of Congress, exists to support Congress in meeting its constitutional responsibilities and to help improve the performance and accountability of the federal government for the American people. GAO examines the use of public funds; evaluates federal programs and policies; and provides analyses, recommendations, and other assistance to help Congress make informed oversight, policy, and funding decisions. GAO's commitment to good government is reflected in its core values of accountability, integrity, and reliability.[63]

Two GAO reports will be referenced within this thesis, both pertaining to Congressional follow-up of DoD activities resulting from the 2001 Space Commission findings.

---

[62] Department of the Air Force. *Air Force Operational Tactics, Techniques, and Procedures 2-3.4, Joint Space Operations Center (Draft)*. 20 January 2006.

[63] United States. Report to Congressional Committees: *DEFENSE SPACE ACTIVITIES: Additional Actions Needed to Implement Human Capital Strategy and Develop Space Personnel*. Government Accountability Office. August 2004. p. 29. http://www.gao.gov/new.items/d04697.pdf. June 2007.

9. **Space and Naval Warfare Systems Command (SPAWAR)**

SPAWAR and its five systems centers provide much of the tactical and non-tactical information management technology required by the Navy to complete its operational missions. Space and Naval Warfare Systems Center San Diego (SSC San Diego) is the U.S. Navy's research, development, test and evaluation, engineering and fleet support center for command, control and communication systems and ocean surveillance. SSC San Diego provides information resources to support the joint warfighter in mission execution and force protection.[64]

10. **Program Executive Officer (PEO) Space Systems**

The Program Executive Officer for Space Systems (PEO Space Systems) is a Navy Echelon II acquisition organization charted by the secretary of the Navy to manage and procure narrowband communications satellites in support of the Department of Defense (DoD). The PEO Space Systems organization was formally established 5 May 2004. The PEO Space Systems Headquarters staff is located in Chantilly, Virginia, with additional staff members located in San Diego, California.

The PEO Space Systems mission is to develop, acquire, integrate, produce, launch, test, and provide operational support to reliable, affordable, flexible, effective, and seamless space systems that support DoD and U.S. Agencies to enable joint, coalition, combined, and Naval operations. The PEO Space Systems coordinates all Department of the Navy (DoN) space research, development, and acquisition activities.

The PEO Space System reports to the Assistant Secretary of the Navy for Research, Development, and Acquisition (ASN(RDA)) for executing acquisition responsibilities for assigned programs. The PEO Space Systems provides executive management and oversight to the Communications Satellite Program Office (PMW-146) for assigned Leased Satellite (LEASAT), Ultra High Frequency (UFO) Follow-On (UFO), and Mobile User Objective System (MUOS) satellite communications (SATCOM) programs. Additionally, the PEO Space Systems serve as the DoN's space program executive officer as called for in the DoD National Security Space Acquisition Policy (NSSAP) 03-01, reporting to the Under Secretary of the Air Force as DoD Executive Agent for Space and Milestone Decision Authority for major space acquisition

---

[64] Department of the Navy. *Space and Naval Warfare Systems Command Center San Diego.* http://www.spawar.navy.mil/sandiego/. June 2007.

matters and programs. The PEO Space Systems reports to the chief of Naval Operations (CNO) and Commandant Marine Corps (CMC), through the Commander, Space and Naval Warfare Systems Command (SPAWAR), for matters pertaining to in-service support for its assigned programs. The Program Executive Officer also provides a unique interface to other national security space organizations through his concurrent assignments as Commander, SPAWAR Space Field Activity (SSFA) and as Director, Communications Directorate, National reconnaissance Office (NRO), enabling a continuing partnership and effective integration of space systems expertise and best practices across the Navy-DoD-Intelligence Community interface.[65]

Figure 2, below, diagrams the command and acquisition relationship of major Navy organizations in the larger national space community.

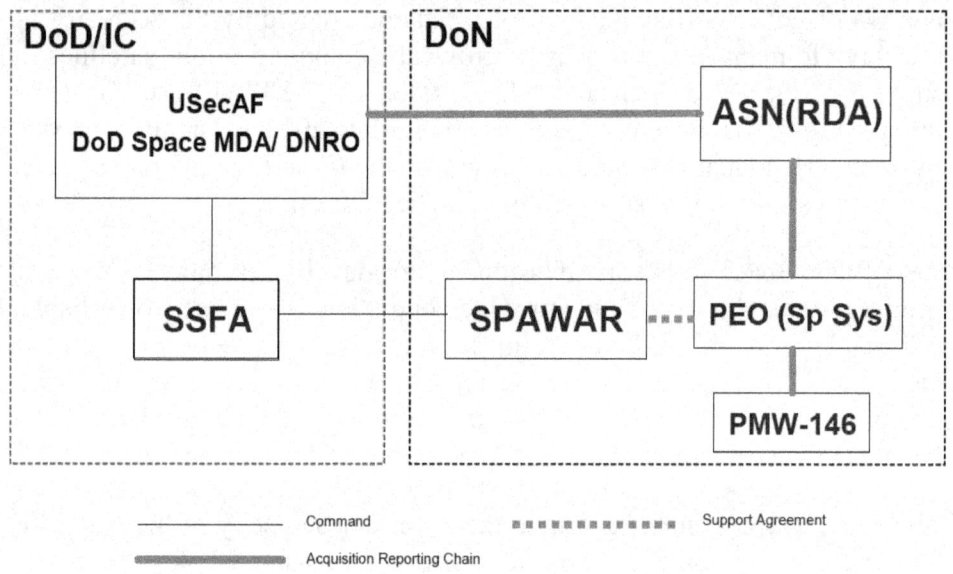

Figure 2.   PEO Space Systems in the Context of Space Systems Acquisition

11. Navy Communications Satellite Program Office (PMW-146)

The mission of the Navy's Communications Satellite Program Office (PMW-146) is to acquire space based communications systems for the fleet and joint users. The Joint Chiefs of Staff's Joint Vision 2020 and

---

[65] Department of the Navy. *PEO Space Systems Missions Statement.* Space and Naval Warfare Systems Command. http://enterprise.spawar.navy.mil/body.cfm?type=c&category=26&subcat=54. May 2007.

Chief of Naval Operations' Information Technology for the 21st Century (IT-21) provide the strategic direction for future acquisitions. PMW-146 is the Navy's only major buyer of communications satellites, building on a strong and successful heritage of the Navy in Space, including FLTSAT, LEASAT, and the UHF Follow-On (UFO) programs. PMW-146 is continuing to satisfy the warfighters' emerging communication requirements using innovative military and commercial technology advances. Launching one more UFO satellite in 2003, the present UFO constellation will continue to provide UHF, SHF, EHF communications and Ka Global Broadcast Service well into the new millennium. PMW-146 is a dynamic example of acquisition reform and a proven award winning advocate of commercial partnering and cooperative ventures to streamline acquisition.[66]

12. National Reconnaissance Office (NRO)

The NRO designs, builds and operates the nation's reconnaissance satellites. NRO products, provided to an expanding list of customers like the Central Intelligence Agency (CIA) and the Department of Defense (DoD), can warn of potential trouble spots around the world, help plan military operations, and monitor the environment. As part of the 16-member Intelligence Community, the NRO plays a primary role in achieving information superiority for the U. S. Government and Armed Forces. A DoD agency, the NRO is staffed by DoD and CIA personnel. It is funded through the National Reconnaissance Program, part of the National Foreign Intelligence Program.[67]

13. Naval Research Laboratory (NRL)

NRL is the corporate research laboratory for the Navy and Marine Corps and conducts a broad program of scientific research, technology and advanced development. NRL has served the Navy and the nation for over 80 years and continues to meet the complex technological challenges of today's world. The NRL has five site locations, all of which work to field new, innovative technologies for the fleet.[68]

---

[66] Department of the Navy. *PMW-146 Mission Statement.* Space and Naval Warfare Systems Command. 31 May 2007. http://enterprise.spawar.navy.mil/pd14/PMW146/Mission/mission_statement.htm

[67] National Reconnaissance Office. *NRO Vision and Mission Statement.* http://www.nro.gov/. May 2007.

[68] Department of the Navy. *NRL Missions Statement.* Naval Research Lab. http://www.nrl.navy.mil/content.php?P=MISSION. June 2007.

14. Navy Center for Space Technology (NCST)

In its role to preserve and enhance a strong space technology base and provide expert assistance in the development and acquisition of space systems that support naval missions, the activities in Naval Center for Space Technology extend from basic and applied research through advanced development in all areas of interest to the Navy Space program. These activities include developing spacecraft, systems using these spacecraft, and ground command and control stations. Principal functions of the Center include understanding and clarifying requirements; recognizing and prosecuting promising research and development; analyzing and testing systems to quantify their capabilities; developing operational concepts that exploit new technical capabilities; system engineering to allocate design requirements to subsystems; and engineering development and initial operation to test and evaluate selected spacecraft subsystems and systems. The Center is a focal point and integrator for those divisions at NRL whose technologies are used in space systems. The Center also provides systems engineering and technical direction assistance to system acquisition managers of major space systems. In this role, technology transfer is a major goal and motivates a continuous search for new technologies and capabilities and the development of prototypes that demonstrate the integration of such technologies.[69]

B. CONCEPTS

1. Sea Power 21

The 21st century is clearly characterized by dangerous uncertainty and conflict. In this unpredictable environment, military forces will be required to defeat a growing range of conventional and asymmetric threats.

"Sea Power 21" is the Navy's vision to align, organize, integrate, and transform to meet the challenges that lie ahead. It requires us to continually and aggressively reach. It is global in scope, fully joint in execution, and dedicated to transformation. It reinforces and expands concepts being pursued by the other services—long-range strike; global intelligence, surveillance, and reconnaissance; expeditionary maneuver warfare; and light, agile ground forces—to generate maximum combat power from the joint team.

---

[69] Department of the Navy. *Navy Center for Space Technology Mission Statement*. Naval Research Lab. http://www.ncst.nrl.navy.mil/HomePage/Mission.html. June 2007.

"Sea Power 21" will employ current capabilities in new ways, introduce innovative capabilities as quickly as possible, and achieve unprecedented maritime power. Decisive warfighting capabilities from the sea will be built around:

Sea Strike—expanded power projection that employs networked sensors, combat systems, and warriors to amplify the offensive impact of sea-based forces;

Sea Shield—global defensive assurance produced by extended homeland defense, sustained access to littorals, and the projection of defensive power deep overland;

Sea Basing—enhanced operational independence and support for joint forces provided by networked, mobile, and secure sovereign platforms operating in the maritime domain.

ForceNet is the "glue" that binds together Sea Strike, Sea Shield, and Sea Basing. It is the operational construct and architectural framework for naval warfare in the information age, integrating warriors, sensors, command and control, platforms, and weapons into a networked, distributed combat force.

The powerful warfighting capabilities of "Sea Power 21" will ensure our joint force dominates the unified battlespace of the 21st century, strengthening America's ability to assure friends, deter adversaries, and triumph over enemies—anywhere, anytime.[70]

2. Coordinating Authority

The Unified Actions Armed Forces Joint Publication 0-2 defines Coordinating Authority as:

A commander or individual assigned responsibility for coordinating specific functions or activities involving forces of two or more Military Departments, two or more joint force components or two or more forces of the same Service. The commander or individual has the authority to require consultation between the agencies involved, but does not have the authority to compel agreement.[71]

---

[70] Vern Clark, Admiral, U.S. Navy. *Sea Power 21. Projecting Decisive Joint Capabilities*. Naval Institute Proceedings. October 2002. http://www.navy.mil/navydata/cno/proceedings.html. June 2007.

[71] United States. *Joint Publication 0-2: Unified Action Armed Forces (UNAAF)*. Department of Defense, Joint Staff. Washington D.C.: U.S. Government Printing Office. GL-6.

3. Space Authority

To facilitate unity of the theater/joint operations area (JOA) space effort, the supported combatant commander or a joint force commander (JFC) may designate a space authority. The space authority will coordinate space operations, integrate space capabilities, and have primary responsibility for in-theater joint space operations planning. The coordinating authority typically will be the joint force air component commander, joint force land component commander, or joint force maritime component commander. In this position, the space authority designated by the JFC will coordinate space support of established objectives and act on behalf of the combatant commander with primary responsibility in theater for joint space operations planning.[72]

4. Space Coordinating Authority (SCA)

The Joint Force Commander within a specified theater, area of responsibility or operation will delegate space coordinating authority to the component commander with the biggest play and expertise in space. This component commander has always been the Air Force, thus the J/CFACC is usually designated the space coordinating authority within the theater, AOR or operation. The JFC still maintains overall space authority control at the Joint Task Force level. Responsibilities of the SCA include:[73]

- Determine, deconflict, and prioritize military space requirements for the JTF.
- Recommend appropriate command relationships for space to the JFC.
- Help facilitate space target nomination.
- Maintain space situational awareness.
- Request space inputs from JTF staff and components during planning.
- Ensure optimum interoperability of space assets with coalition forces.
- Recommend JTF military space requirement priorities to JFC.

---

[72] United States. Joint Staff. *Joint Publication 3-14: Joint Doctrine for Space Operations*. Department of Defense. p. ix. http://www.dtic.mil/doctrine/jel/new_pubs/jp3_14.pdf. June 2007.

[73] Department of the Air Force. *Air Force Doctrine Document 2, Operations and Organizations*. Washington D.C.: Government Printing Office, 27 June 2006. pp. 62-63.

5. **Joint Warfighting Space (JWS)**

The JWS concept features the delivery of responsive space and near-space (i.e., area above the earth from ~ 65,000 to 325,000 feet altitude, sub-orbital) capabilities to directly support the joint force commander (JFC) in a theater across the range of military operations, with emphasis at the operational and tactical warfighting levels. It is envisioned as a rapid reaction, networked set of space and near-space capabilities dedicated to the JFC and integrated with National Security Space (NSS) and organic theater systems.[74] Figure 3 shows the envisioned JWS concept.

The Joint Warfighter Space organization will require dedicated, knowledgeable and well educated Navy space cadre personnel to ensure Navy needs and requirements are met.

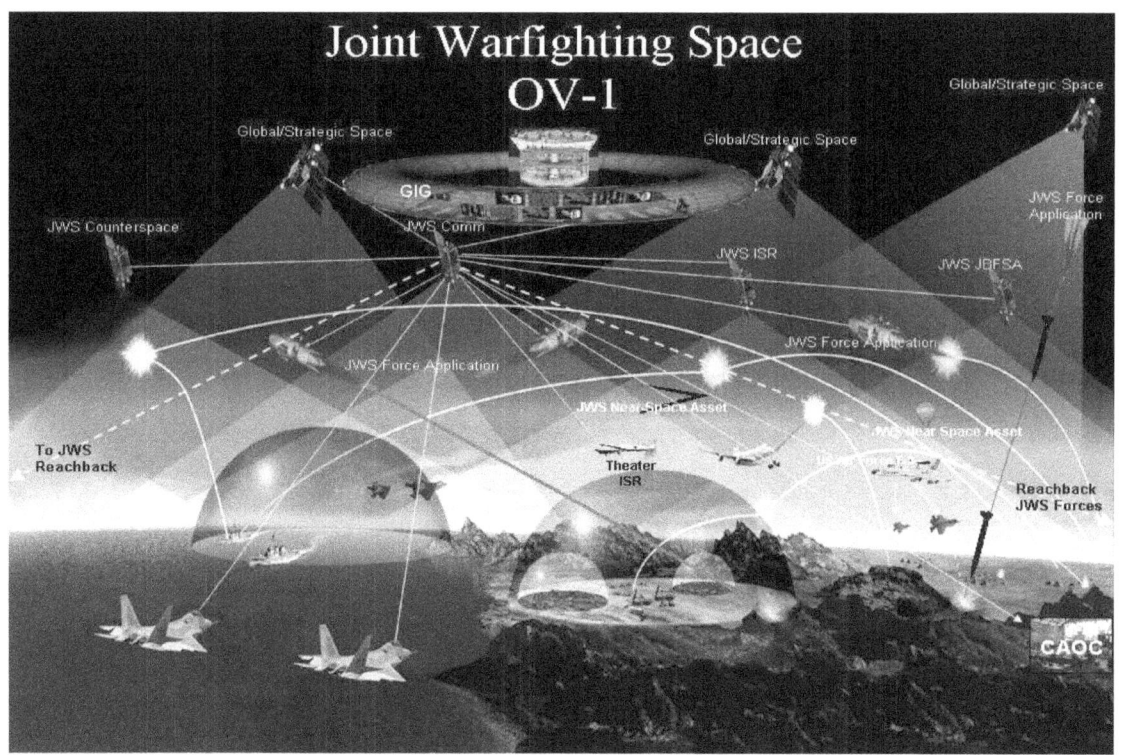

Figure 3. Joint Warfighter Space Operational Vision[75]

---

[74] Department of the Air Force. *Operating Concept for Joint Warfighting Space (Draft)*. 13 Jan 2005. p. 1.

[75] Department of the Air Force. *Operating Concept for Joint Warfighting Space (Draft)*. 13 Jan 2005. p. 15.

6. Space Effects and Space Effects Packages

Though these terms are interpreted in many ways, an effect is simply something designed to produce a distinctive or desired impression. A space effect is the utilization of both space force application and enhancement to provide the warfighter and/or commander with necessary products to ensure mission success. In the Fleet, space effects are outlined and produced through the use of the Space Effects Package (SEP). This SEP is defined within the Fleet Space Handbook as "a systematic process that applies all available Space capabilities to support Strike Group operations."[76] The SEP process consists of a Space Assessment and Space Operations Plan.

> The Space Assessment considers the following: Space System Status, Space Weather, GPS and SATCOM EMI, and Space Vulnerabilities. The Space Operations Plan takes the Space Assessment and Strike Group mission requirements to tailor a plan for use of all space capabilities to support the mission.[77]

Knowledge gained from exposure to the definitions and concepts that encompass the United States Navy space efforts provides a functional baseline of understanding for future arguments contained in follow-on chapters within this thesis. Comprehension and recognition of space terminology and conceptual ideology are necessary to appreciate the full effect of these arguments. In addition, exposure to the numerous and sometimes confusing Navy space policy documents and instructions is also necessary to ensure desired effects are achieved when pondering the proposed argument of redefining Navy space efforts.

---

[76] Department of the Navy. Naval Network Warfare Command. *Fleet Space Handbook.*8. 2007. p. 13.
[77] Ibid., p. 13.

III. U.S. NAVY SPACE CAMPAIGN

Between 2003 and 2007, the United States Navy's space efforts have undergone a significant transformation as the organization attempts to maintain space support to the operational maritime domain in a network-centric warfare environment. As stated in the 2005 Naval Space Campaign Plan, "The Naval Space Campaign is operational and aggressive, focused on delivering space capabilities to the warfighter to increase combat effectiveness."[78] This chapter will investigate the origins and evolution of the Naval Space Campaign, focusing on the policies that help generate it, the current status of the campaign, and the future efforts implied by the Naval Space Campaign.

A. POLICY

1. Background and Current Policies

The evolution of the current Naval Space Campaign can be traced to the 2001 Space Commission findings and the after-effects felt throughout the Department of Defense with regards to those findings. From a doctrine and policy perspective, Department of Defense Directive 5101.2, dated June 3, 2003, designated the Air Force as Department of Defense Executive Agent for Space. Secretary of Defense Memorandum dated October 18, 2001, Subject: National Security Space Management and Organization, tasked Secretaries of the Military Departments to, "maintain a sufficient cadre of space qualified professionals…to ensure each Service retains the ability to develop, plan, program, and acquire space systems uniquely required by individual service missions."[79] In July 2002, the CNO approved the establishment of a Navy Space Cadre and directed funding for that endeavor.

---

[78] Department of the Navy. *Naval Space Campaign Plan 2005-2007 'Space Capabilities for the Warfighter'*. Naval Network Warfare Command. 13 November 2005. pp. 3-4.

[79] Ibid., p. 4.

a. *SECNAVINST 5400.39C (April 6, 2004)*

On April 6th, 2004, the Secretary of the Navy officially released the Department of the Navy Space Policy (SECNAVINST 5400.39C):

> The United States Navy and Marine Corps must maintain their ability to tactically exploit the capabilities provided by space systems and participate in all appropriate aspects of the changed NSS environment in order to function as an integrated member of the Nation's joint warfighting team...the DoN must continually reassess its approach and investment to ensure that naval forces receive the maximum benefit of space-based capabilities.[80]

The SECNAVINST describes the need for "DoN space requirements to be represented at joint deliberations on future space systems...provide the resources and manpower necessary to formulate, articulate and defend naval requirements for space."[81] It further acknowledged the need for DoN Space representation in the joint processes for space system architecture and requirements development:

> To achieve its space goals, the DoN will recruit, educate, qualify, and retain a professional space cadre...DoN Space Cadre personnel will compete for all appropriate senior leadership positions in joint, national, and naval space programs and organizations.[82]

The instruction also notes that DoN representation must also be present within the joint and National space arena - to include establishing a mutually beneficial relationship with the DoD Executive Agent for Space. To this end, the instruction clearly favors the need for a robust and competent Navy Space Cadre, one capable of accomplishing the above mentioned requirements. Of note, when discussing the Navy's need to acquire, control and fly their own satellites, the instruction states: "*When appropriate*, developing, acquiring, and operating space-based assets and associated

---

[80] Department of the Navy. SECNAV Instruction 5400.39C: *Department of Navy Space Policy*. 6 April 2004. p. 2. http://ftp.fas.org/irp/doddir/navy/secnavinst/5400_39c.pdf. April 2007.

[81] Ibid., pp. 3-4.

[82] Ibid., pp. 3-4.

capabilities to satisfy joint, national, or naval operational requirements."[83] Liberal interpretation of this verbiage lends credence to an organizational structure that permits the Navy to focus the majority of its space program efforts on establishing, educating and maintaining a robust Navy Space Cadre, even at the expense of operating it's own space-based assets - identified as relevant only 'when appropriate' in this instruction.

b. *CJCSI 6250.01B (May 28, 2004)*

This Joint Chiefs of Staff Instruction outlines the use and management of all DoD SATCOM. Explicit in the instruction is direction to the Services regarding use and management of DoD controlled communication satellites. It mandates impartial treatment and consideration for use of assets and prohibits the notion that the more satellites an individual Service acquires or operates, the more SATCOM time and allocation they will receive. "This instruction provides high-level, operational policy, guidance and procedures for the planning, management, employment and use of satellite communications (SATCOM) resources for the Department of Defense."[84] The instruction also provides a SATCOM priority table in which the Joint Chiefs of Staff directs the precedence of use for communication satellites. Again, no preference in operation is given to the agency holding asset ownership.

c. *Navy Space Cadre Human Capital Strategy (December 2004)*

"Successful application of space in the Navy translates to a healthy and robust Navy Space Cadre."[85] In response to the SECNAVINST 5400.39C directive for the establishment of a Navy Space Cadre, in December of 2004, the DoN released its Human Capital Strategy for the implementation of this new cadre.

---

[83] Department of the Navy. SECNAV Instruction 5400.39C: *Department of Navy Space Policy*. 6 April 2004. pp. 3-4. http://ftp.fas.org/irp/doddir/navy/secnavinst/5400_39c.pdf. April 2007. Emphasis added.

[84] Chairman of the Joint Chiefs of Staff. CJCSI 6250.01B: *Satellite Communications*. 28 May 2004. p. 1.

[85] Department of the Navy. *Navy Space Cadre Human Capital Strategy, Version 1.1*. 27. Naval Network Warfare Command. December 2004. p. 1.

This HCS supports and complements the National Security Space's Human Capital Resource Strategy (HCRS) dated February 2004 and the DoN HCS dated June 2004. The objective of the Space Cadre HCS is to groom and shape the workforce to fill major decision-making positions across the Navy, Joint, and National Security Space assessment, requirements, science & technology/research & development, acquisition, and operational arena in order to maximize return on investment in meeting evolving Naval requirements...Proper management and placement of Navy Space Cadre personnel will allow the Navy to gain huge return on investment and leverage more than $12B per year spent on unclassified space systems by the Air Force and other services.[86]

d. *OPNAVINST 5400.43 (May 20, 2005)*

This CNO instruction was implemented to establish procedures and clarify roles and responsibilities for implementing the Department of the Navy Space Policy per SECNAVINST 5400.39C.[87] Contained within the discussion section of this instruction is the description of the Navy Space Cadre. "Success is dependent on a solid foundation of Space Cadre and a forward leaning Navy Space Team that actively coordinates Navy space needs, priorities, and innovative capabilities within the Navy, the wider NSS and the civil space community."[88]

The policy set forth in OPNAVINST 5400.43 consists of three distinctive sections – the Navy will:

i) Integrate the essential capabilities provided by space systems at every appropriate level throughout the naval force;

ii) Shape the outcome of joint deliberations on future space capabilities to ensure the combat effectiveness of naval force; and

iii) Recruit, educate, qualify, and retain a professional space cadre.[89]

---

[86] Department of the Navy. *Navy Space Cadre Human Capital Strategy, Version 1.1.* Naval Network Warfare Command. 27 December 2004. p.2.

[87] Department of the Navy. OPNAVINST 5400.43A *Navy Space Policy Implementation.* 12 February 2007. p. 2.
https://doni.daps.dla.mil/Directives/Forms/AllItems.aspx?RootFolder=%2fDirectives%2f05000%20General%20Management%20Security%20and%20Safety%20Services%2f05%2d400%20Organization%20and%20Functional%20Support%20Services. May 2007.

[88] Ibid., p. 3.

[89] Ibid., p. 3.

The Deputy CNO (Manpower and Personnel/CNO N1) is responsible for managing the Navy Space Cadre to include designating the Navy Space Cadre Advisor to act in a virtual community manager role for the Space Cadre. Naval Network Warfare Command is responsible for review and formulation of Navy Space Policy, oversight of Navy space activities, and is designated as the Space Type Commander and Space Functional Authority per SECNAVINST 5400.39C. NETWARCOM is also responsible for developing, maintaining and overseeing the Navy Space Human Capital Strategy...coordinating with the fleet on best distribution of space expertise in afloat billets. Furthermore, this instruction identifies NETWARCOM as the United States Navy functional component to USSTRATCOM for Space. Supporting USSTRATCOM functional component for JFCC Space as required.[90] The wording of this instruction suggests a number of interpretations. One suggestion is a clear and unmistakable requirement for an established, educated and robust Navy Space Cadre. Less concrete is direction provided regarding Navy requirements or benefits to be gained from internal acquisition and operation of space systems.

On February 12, 2007 the CNO released OPNAVINST 5400.43A. Only a few changes were added to the original instruction, primarily focusing on space effects integration into the FORCEnet architecture.

e. *Naval Space Campaign Plan 2005-2007 (November 13, 2005)*

The Naval Space Campaign Plan was published in an effort to further clarify and officially establish the Navy's policy and guidance with regards to naval space efforts.

> The Naval Space Campaign is fleet-centric, designed to improve space processes across the naval enterprise. To best accomplish this, Naval Space Campaign efforts are synchronized with naval space strategy development and the Navy Space Cadre Human Capital Strategy. The Naval Space Campaign serves as a forcing function for the naval space

---

[90] Department of the Navy. OPNAVINST 5400.43A *Navy Space Policy Implementation*. 12 February 2007. p. 8.
https://doni.daps.dla.mil/Directives/Forms/AllItems.aspx?RootFolder=%2fDirectives%2f05000%20General%20Management%20Security%20and%20Safety%20Services%2f05%2d400%20Organization%20and%20Functional%20Support%20Services. May 2007.

strategy and is dependent upon the space cadre human capital strategy to put the right space skill set in the right place at the right time.[91]

The objectives contained within the plan are critical to the current and future success of fleet operations around the globe.[92]

- Develop Maritime-specific Space Requirements: Develop space requirements based on current capabilities and limitations of space systems.

- Satisfy Maritime Requirements: Ensure space systems provided by the EA for Space and National Security Space sector provide desired effects to meet maritime requirements, and provide feedback through the Naval Capabilities Development Process if they do not.

- Increase Space Knowledge: Promote a better understanding in the fleet of how space-provided effects support maritime operations and scheme of maneuver.

- Improve Combat Effectiveness: Improve fleet combat effectiveness with smarter, more aggressive use of space-based capabilities, focusing on maximizing effects for the Carrier Strike Group.

- Improve Human Capital: Cultivate Navy Space Cadre expertise for assignment into joint space and National Security Space (NSS) billets.

- Ingrain Cultural Change: Harvest space-related best practices from Naval Space Campaign lessons learned and institutionalize them through doctrine and policy.

- Understand Space System Vulnerabilities: Ensure Navy seniors understand the vulnerabilities of space systems and mitigation options.

Like the OPNAV and SECNAV Instructions, the Navy Space Campaign Plan does not explicitly mention the requirement for the U.S. Navy to acquire, operate, control or perform management of narrow-band communications satellites or resources.

The foundation of the Naval Space Campaign is the expertise and professional knowledge of the Navy and Marine Corps Space Cadre. Success is dependent on a solid foundation of Navy Space Cadre…that

---

[91] Department of the Navy. *Naval Space Campaign Plan 2005-2007 'Space Capabilities for the Warfighter'*. Naval Network Warfare Command. 13 November 2005. pp. 3-4.

[92] Ibid., p. 8.

actively coordinates naval space needs, priorities, and innovative capabilities with the Navy, Marine Corps, the wider NSS and the civil space community.[93]

NETWARCOM is currently working on a "Navy Space Concept of Operations" (CONOPS) document that will supersede the Navy Space Campaign Plan. This document is currently in draft format and not available for public consumption.

f. U.S. National Space Policy (August 31, 2006)

"The president authorized a new national space policy on August 31, 2006 that establishes overarching national policy that governs the conduct of U.S. space activities."[94] Just like the SECNAVINST 5400.39C, OPNAVINST 5400.43 and the Naval Space Campaign Plan, the President ordered the development of space professionals to ensure the United States continues to sustain excellence within the dominion of space. "Develop Space Professionals...Department and agencies that conduct space related activities shall establish standards and implement activities to develop and maintain highly skilled, experienced, and motivated space professionals within their workforce."[95]

2. Positive Aspects of the Navy's Space Policy

There are many constructive features in the prose of recent Navy Space documents and policies: Establishment of a Navy Space TYCOM; Establishment of the Navy Space Cadre; Increases in space effects awareness throughout the fleet; Inception of the CSG Space Officer; and initial publication of the Fleet Space Handbook.

The designation of NETWARCOM as the Navy's Space Type Commander has the potential to be a significant step forward for Navy space efforts in the presence of a space-savvy commander. As a three-star admiral, NETWARCOM has more influence

---

[93]Department of the Navy. *Naval Space Campaign Plan 2005-2007 'Space Capabilities for the Warfighter'*. Naval Network Warfare Command. 13 November 2005. p. 14.

[94] United States. *United States National Space Policy*. 31 August 2006. http://www.ostp.gov/html/US%20National%20Space%20Policy.pdf. May 2007. p. 1.

[95] Ibid., p 3.

than has been previously fielded in the Naval space community. This promotion of command allows for greater representation of Navy space efforts not only in the naval arena, but in the joint and national space environment as well.

Another positive aspect to the composition and publication of these policy documents is that both SECNAVINST 5400.39C and OPNAVINST 5400.43 provide the naval forces much-needed definition of responsibilities with regards to Naval space activities. Supporting that guidance is the creation and direction of the Navy Space Cadre. The Navy Space Cadre Human Capital Strategy and the Naval Space Campaign Plan both outline the need for a vigorous and hearty Navy Space Cadre and enunciate the benefits that could be realized with the development of this type of core space proponent.

Finally, the policies paved the way for the first-ever CSG Space Officer. The results of this experiment have not been officially released, but preliminary indications point to notable successes for the implementation of space effects at the operational level, and validation of the concept of a "space-enabled staff."[96]

3. Negative Aspects of the Navy's Space Policy

The Navy's space policies and plans lack sufficient clarity as to the current structure, status, ownership and operation of Navy controlled satellites. Further, there are omissions regarding the articulation of naval usage and allocation of unclassified space assets, to include commercial communications satellites. Though not always contained in high-level policy, correction of these omissions could have been incorporated within the Naval Space Campaign Plan 2005-2007 as an effort to provide the target audience with an opportunity to understand the current and future status of naval space activity.

Another shortcoming in the campaign is the absence of a consolidated Navy space command and control architecture. Confusion and uncertainty are rampant when trying to discern a possible flow of command and control for operations, effects, acquisition and requirements definition.

---

[96] Zigmond Leszczynski, Commander, U.S. Navy. *EISENHOWER Strike Group (IKESG) End-of-Deployment Report, Space Segment.* Carrier Strike Group 8. May 2007.

These policies are also lacking significantly in direct guidance relating to an implementation strategy for the establishment and maintenance of a robust Navy Space Cadre. The Naval Space Campaign Plan, DoD Directive 5101.2 (DoD Executive Agent for Space), OPNAV Instruction 5400.43 (Navy Space Policy Implementation) and SECNAV Instruction 5400.39 (Department of the Navy Space Policy) all mandate a "sufficient cadre of space-qualified personnel", but no instruction is given regarding the execution of that objective.

Similarly, insufficient instruction and guidance in the realm of joint space endeavors are available. Though not clearly identified as critical to the service, the Navy's role in the joint space sector is worthy of at least honorary mention. Again the Navy's space policies, procedures and instructions are deficient in their ability to provide guidance and direction in the joint space effort. This is one of the greatest shortcomings of the Navy's space policy as the entire DoD conducts business within the joint-centric arena.

These failings in policy pose an impediment to the success of the Navy Space Campaign. The lack of guidance and direction, in conjunction with platitudes regarding network centric warfare and party-line rhetoric, needs to be addressed and reevaluated by senior Navy leadership. In order to assure success in current and future Navy Space operations, leadership must jump-start space requirements and processes with a critical revision of Naval Space policy.

B. NAVY SPACE CAMPAIGN COMMAND AND CONTROL CONSTRUCT

Though the SECNAV and OPNAV instructions mentioned above clearly define the roles and responsibilities of those directorates which control the different space elements, the overall Navy-wide space Command and Control (C^2) hierarchy and organizational graphic representation have never been formally published. The current C^2 for Navy space is one of the most perplexing, splintered and continually evolving of all force architectures under the purview of the U.S. Navy. Figure 4, below, is a simplified reporting structure specific to the Naval Satellite Operations Center, and represents one of the only historical command relationship organization charts available in this field.

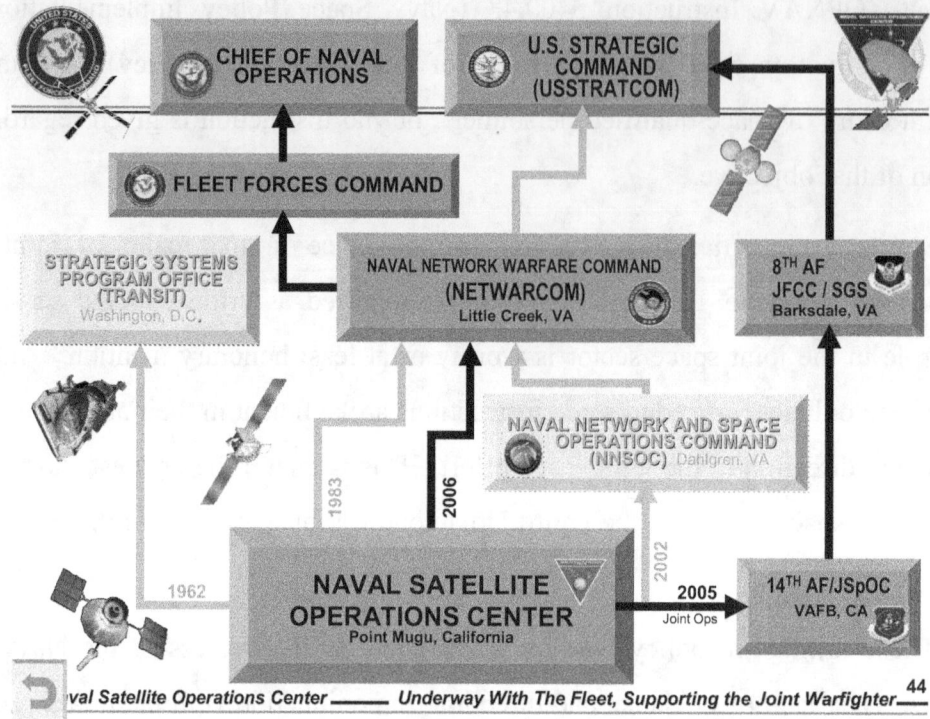

Figure 4. C² Historical Flow Chart for the Naval Satellite Operations Center[97]

This diagram illustrates the transformation of just one of the numerous Navy space components.

Instead of spotlighting the traditional C² methods within the Navy space realm, the next section will focus on the C² of Space effects in an effort to understand how those effects get to the warfighter and how Navy Space Cadre representation within that C² structure plays a critical role in the success of naval space effects. "Knowledge of how space effects get to the CSG and ESG is critical to ensuring warfighters have required space effects."[98] Figure 5 (below) shows the current C² flow for supplying space effects

---

[97] Paul M. Insch, Captain, U.S. Navy. *NAVSOC Command Brief*. Naval Satellite Operations Center. PowerPoint Brief. June 2006. Slide 44.

[98] Department of the Navy. *Naval Space Campaign Plan 2005-2007 'Space Capabilities for the Warfighter'*. Naval Network Warfare Command. 13 November 2005. p. 10.

to the operational naval warfighter. CSG-8, the fleet Executive Agent for the Navy Space Campaign, returned from a milestone deployment in May of 2007, during which they used this structure to ensure that space effects were maximized.

CSG-8 C2 Space Effects Operational Flow

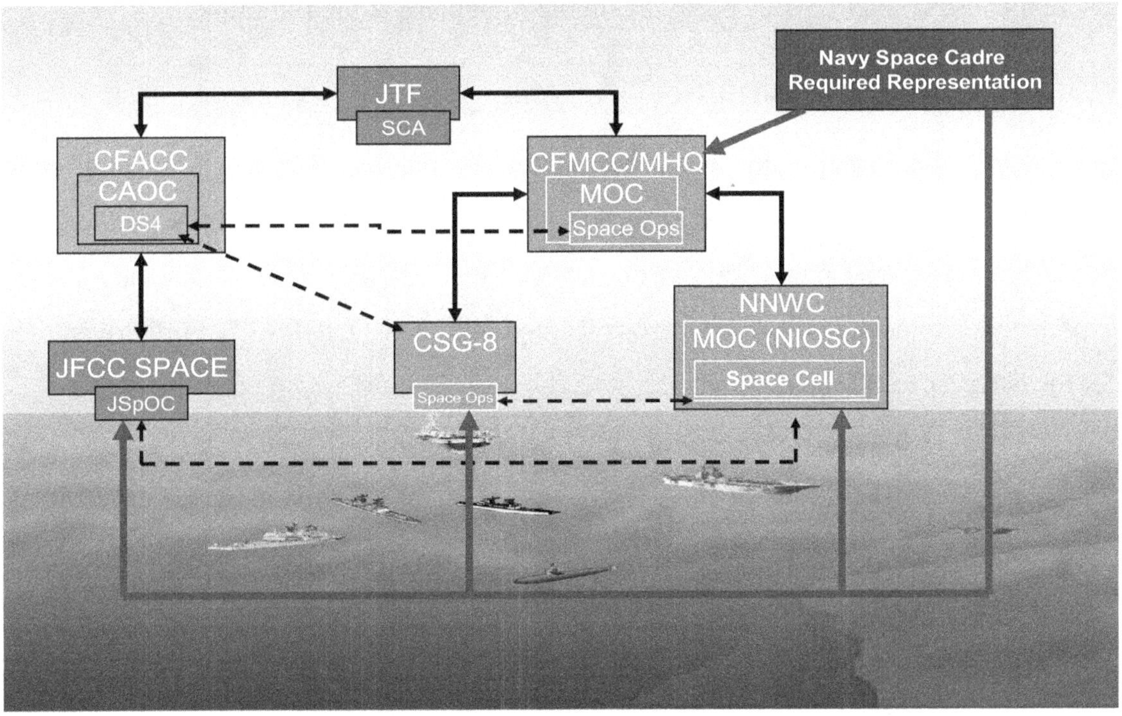

Figure 5. CSG-8 C² Space Effects Operational Flow Chart modified by authors to reflect Navy Space Cadre Representation Requirements[99]

The official End-of-Deployment Report for CSG-8 is a classified document published and located on the SIPRNET CSG-8 homepage. The lessons learned from this endeavor will be incorporated in the new Navy Space CONOPS tentatively scheduled to be released by the end of 2007. The benefits from this C² Space Effects construct were identified as essential to CSG-8's incorporation of space effects into daily operations.

> CSG-8/IKESG has benefited greatly from our journey as the fleet EA for space. We are smarter towards our use of space capabilities and better recognize our vulnerabilities in that regard as well. As such we are better prepared to prevail in conflict. While deployed in the CENTCOM AOR,

---

[99] Julie Niedermaier, Commander, U.S. Navy. *Navy Space Cadre Update (SSFA Space Indoctrination)*. PowerPoint Brief. March 2007. Slide 19.

Commander, IKESG could say with confidence that every bit of space capability available was brought to bear in support of designated operational events.[100]

It is important to note that the success of this C^2 construct and the accomplishments of CSG-8 rely heavily on the use and proper staging of Navy Space Cadre members – Navy Space personnel in the right place at the right time.

C. FUTURE ENDEAVORS

One of the major upcoming milestones for the Naval Space Campaign is to officially publish and employ the Fleet Space Operations CONOPS. Some of the delay in the processing and publication is due to NETWARCOM's desire to include CSG-8 experiences and post deployment lessons learned into the CONOPS.[101] Further ventures for the Navy Space Campaign include:

- NIOSC Support through ESG/CSG Work-ups
- Formalization of Navy Space Education and Training
- Space in Turnaround Training Plans (TTP)
- Warfare Commander's Conference
- CSG Space Operations Course
- NSSI Billets dedicated to CSG/ESG Training
- Formalization of Space "Play" in CSG/ESG Fleet Response Training Plan
- Master Scenario Event List (MSEL)/Naval Mission Essential Tasks (NMET) development with Strike Force Training, Atlantic
- Formalization of space "Play" in all Navy exercises
- Posturing to make Joint Forces Maritime Component Commander (JFMCC) the Theater Space Coordinating Authority

Just as the Department of Defense is undergoing a transformation process, so is the Navy's Space Campaign. Within the current construct of the campaign lies the foundation for the Navy Space Cadre, the establishment of a Navy Space TYCOM and

---

[100] Zigmond Leszczynski, Commander, U.S. Navy. *EISENHOWER Strike Group (IKESG) End-of-Deployment Report, Space Segment.* Carrier Strike Group 8. May 2007.

[101] Julie Niedermaier, Commander, U.S. Navy. *Navy Space Cadre Update (SSFA Space Indoctrination).* PowerPoint Brief. March 2007. Slide 20.

the first ever CSG Staff Space Officer. The shortfalls associated with the current campaign reside in its lack of an implementation strategy, ambiguity of intent for Navy space usage, and the Navy's role in the joint space environment. Good, bad or otherwise, the Navy Space Campaign is underway, and only through sound decision making and aggressive leadership will the Navy space community be able to navigate through the troubled waters that lie ahead.

THIS PAGE INTENTIONALLY LEFT BLANK

IV. NAVY SPACE CADRE

The Navy space cadre was founded by order of the Secretary of the Navy on April 6th, 2004[102] as a response to the July 2003 Department of Defense Directive 5101.2, which mandated that:

The Heads of the DoD Components shall:

Develop and maintain a sufficient cadre of space-qualified personnel to support their Component in space planning, programming, acquisition, and operations. Support the DoD Executive Agent for Space with space cadre personnel to represent their Component in DoD-wide planning, programming, and acquisition activities.[103]

The creation of the Navy Space Cadre has been established in a parallel but unequal effort with the Air Force, Army and Marine Corps Space Cadres. The differences among the service efforts in constructing their organizations of "space experts" is instructive as to the assessed cost-benefit relation that each branch assigns to its use of space, and relative leadership understanding of the impact of space effects.

This chapter examines the continuing formation of the Navy's Space Cadre, its expected roles in the National Security Space arena, and a comparison with the organization, roles and responsibilities of the other services' Space Cadres.

A. ORIGIN

1. DoD-wide Policy

The 2001 "Commission to Assess United States National Security Space Management and Organization" (otherwise known as the '2001 Rumsfeld Space Commission,' or '2001 Space Commission') kicked off the most recent round of reorganization within the U.S. Department of Defense Space Community with the following focus and statements:

---

[102] Department of the Navy. SECNAV Instruction 5400.39C: *Department of the Navy Space Policy*. 6 April 2004.

[103] United States. Department of Defense Directive 5101.2, *DoD Executive Agent for Space.* July 2003. Section 6.3.5. http://www.dtic.mil/whs/directives/corres/html/510102.htm. June 2007.

The Commission examined the role of organization and management in developing and implementing national-level guidance and in establishing requirements, acquiring and operating systems, and planning, programming and budgeting for national security space capabilities. The review concentrated on intelligence and military space operations as they relate to the needs of the national leadership as well as the needs of the military in conducting air, land and sea operations and independent space operations.

... while organization and management are important, the critical need is national leadership to elevate space on the national security agenda.[104]

The same document reaches the following conclusion on the subject of organization and management:

Second, the U.S. Government—in particular, the Department of Defense and the Intelligence Community—is not yet arranged or focused to meet the national security space needs of the 21st century. Our growing dependence on space, our vulnerabilities in space and the burgeoning opportunities from space are simply not reflected in the present institutional arrangements. After examining a variety of organizational approaches, the Commission concluded that a number of disparate space activities should promptly be merged, chains of command adjusted, lines of communication opened and policies modified to achieve greater responsibility and accountability. Only then can the necessary trade-offs be made, the appropriate priorities be established and the opportunities for improving U.S. military and intelligence capabilities be realized. Only with senior-level leadership, when properly managed and with the right priorities will U.S. space programs both deserve and attract the funding that is required.[105]

Finally, the following "U.S Objective for Space" is stated:

5. Create and Sustain a Cadre of Space Professionals

Since its inception, a hallmark of the U.S. space program has been worldclass (sic.) scientists, engineers and operators from academic institutions, industry, government agencies and the military Services. Sustained excellence in the scientific and engineering disciplines is

---

[104] United States. *Report of the Commission to Assess United States National Security Space Management and Organization.* Department of Defense. 12 January 2001. p. 5. http://www.dod.mil/pubs/spaceintro.pdf. June 2007.

[105] Ibid., p. 9. This is the second conclusion of five unanimous "matters of key importance" that the authors of the commission reached.

essential to the future of the nation's national security space program. It cannot be taken for granted. Military space professionals will have to master highly complex technology; develop new doctrine and concepts of operations for space launch, offensive and defensive space operations, power projection in, from and through space and other military uses of space; and operate some of the most complex systems ever built and deployed. To ensure the needed talent and experience, the Department of Defense, the Intelligence Community and the nation as a whole must place a high priority on intensifying investments in career development, education and training to develop and sustain a cadre of highly competent and motivated military and civilian space professionals.[106]

Taken together, these positions and statements, as well as other recommendations contained within the 2001 Space Commission document, resulted in Department of Defense Directive 5101.2, released on 3 June 2003. DoDD 5101.2 re-established the Secretary of the Air Force as the Executive Agent for Space (first specified in 1961, DoDD 5160.32, cancelled in 1970) and mandated the creation of individual service component Space Cadres to:

> ...support their Component in space planning, programming, acquisition, and operations. Support the DoD Executive Agent for Space with space cadre personnel to represent their Component in DoD-wide planning, programming, and acquisition activities.[107]

2. The Navy Response

The Navy ostensibly got the jump on the 2003 DoD Directive, with Chief of Naval Operations Admiral Vern Clark approving creation of a "cross-community" Navy Space Cadre in July 2002, following the 2001 Space Commission report. The intent of the Navy Space Cadre effort has been, from the beginning, to function as a strict subspecialty occupation, subordinate to the primary warfare designation or functional area to which the personnel were assigned. The "cross-community" nature of this establishment was proposed as analogous to the Defense Acquisition Community,[108]

---

[106] United States. *Report of the Commission to Assess United States National Security Space Management and Organization.* Department of Defense. 12 January 2001. p. 18. http://www.dod.mil/pubs/spaceintro.pdf. June 2007.

[107] United States. Department of Defense Directive 5101.2, *DoD Executive Agent for Space.* July 2003. Section 6.3.5. http://www.dtic.mil/whs/directives/corres/html/510102.htm. June 2007.

where expertise in the field is acquired through formal educational opportunities and the members of the community move back and forth between tours with their parent warfighting community and tours in the space arena. While consistent with other Navy "subspecialty communities" this method of organization differs substantially from the methods used by the other military services.

The human resources approach to the Space Cadre in the Navy has unfortunately led to a lack of organizational momentum and resultant deficiencies in Human Capital Strategy. These deficiencies were most critically noted in an August 2004 GAO report on the development of Space Personnel.[109] This GAO report identifies Department of Defense efforts in developing and implementing an integration plan for national security space personnel as inadequate, and varying widely by service. More specifically, the 2004 GAO report states that:

> The Air Force and Marine Corps have taken significant actions to develop and manage their space cadres; however, the Army's and Navy's actions have been limited because these two services do not have clear goals and objectives for their space cadres or focal points designated to manage the cadres."[110]

Absence of goals, objectives, and focused action were further identified in the GAO report as stemming from the non-centralized nature of the Navy Space Cadre. The basic concept of space expertise spread across the full variety of Navy warfighting specialties is perceived within the Navy as promoting flexibility and supporting existing promotion paths and policies within individual Space Cadre members' parent communities.[111] Unfortunately, at that time, in 2004, more than two years after the

---

[108] Victor See, Rear Admiral, U.S. Navy. *CHIPS Interview*. CHIPS. January 2006. http://www.chips.navy.mil/archives/06_Jan/web_pages/RADM_SEE.htm. June 2007.

[109] United States. *Report to Congressional Committees: Defense Space Activities: Additional Actions Needed to Implement Human Capital Strategy and Develop Space Personnel*. Government Accountability Office. August 2004. http://www.gao.gov/new.itmes/d04697.pdf. June 2007.

[110] Ibid., p. 3.

[111] Victor See, Rear Admiral, U.S. Navy. *CHIPS Interview*. CHIPS. January 2006. http://www.chips.navy.mil/archives/06_Jan/web_pages/RADM_SEE.htm. June 2007. and:United States. *Transcript of House Armed Services Committee Hearing No. 108–40, Hearing on Space Cadre/Space Professionals*. House of Representatives. One Hundred Eighth Congress, Second Session. 22 July 2004. p. 18. http://commdocs.house.gov/committees/security/has204290.000/has204290_0f.htm. June 2007.

creation of the Navy Space Cadre, the distributed approach to composition of the organization had failed to achieve any of the organizational goals set forth in the 2001 Rumsfeld Space Commission report. Indeed, Navy efforts to formally organize, educate, certify or manage its space personnel, seemed nonexistent. Vice Admiral James McArthur, the commander of the Naval Network Warfare Command (NETWARCOM)[112] at the Space Cadre/Space Professionals House Armed Services Committee hearing on 22 July 2004 was unable to respond in a clear and unambiguous manner to questioning regarding core and critical skills,[113] certification procedures,[114] and general organization and leadership of the Navy Space Cadre.

B. COMPARISONS -- OTHER DOD SPACE CADRE

The individual services each approach the issue of their Space Professional communities differently, but the Navy strays farthest from the other three branches. The Navy decision to forego a specific community and designation for space qualified personnel resulted in a dilution of institutional support for the mission, absence of quantifiable processes for the organization, and absence of appropriate funding. Only in the Navy are space-trained personnel not routinely assigned to space-related positions or belong to a Space Cadre that has the authority to assign personnel to specific positions. Instead, Navy Space Cadre members move into space jobs only as their career progression in their parent community permits. Assignment to a space-coded billet is implicitly secondary to the requirements of an individual's warfighting specialty. At the opposite end of the spectrum, the Air Force has an established career path for personnel from initial accession through retirement. Space is considered a career-field unto itself, and therefore has the established policies and procedures that are expected of a standardized organization. This approach, however, has not necessarily yielded a

---

[112] NETWARCOM is the U.S. Navy organization charged with command and control of Navy space efforts and programs.

[113] United States. *Transcript of House Armed Services Committee Hearing No. 108–40, Hearing on Space Cadre/Space Professionals.* House of Representatives. One Hundred Eighth Congress, Second Session. 22 July 2004. p. 18. http://commdocs.house.gov/committees/security/has204290.000/has204290_0f.htm. June 2007.

[114] Ibid., p. 24.

pervasive and uniform level of operational expertise throughout the Air Force's space cadre. The mindset of many Air Force space operators reflects an institutional focus on the term "operational" as pertaining to controlling, maintaining and operating satellites and their attendant systems. Without exposure to kinetic warfare and combat experience, space "operators" can be prone to miss the boat with regards to terrestrial warfighter requirements and needs.[115] Remediation of problems caused by this lack of satellite operator warfighting acumen must occur on the ground, usually in theater, through the efforts of experienced space products users like Army FA-40s and Marine Corps Space Cadre members. Perhaps as a consequence of the extreme differences between the Air Force and Navy approaches to space cadre, the Army and Marine Corps take an approach somewhere between these two poles, sourcing their officer space expertise at the mid-grade level, after service in another, more fundamental career track. Both the Marines and Army establish a new Military Occupational Specialty for space-savvy officers, and for Army FA-40s, once assigned to the services' Space Cadre, the remainder of their service time is spent in that functional area. The Army, especially, has developed a robust and integrated program for the use of their FA-40 space cadre members, defining theater-level space support requirements and job descriptions, as well as concepts of operation for organic and attached space team assets.[116] This clear and careful establishment of roles and responsibilities for Army space personnel seems to stem not only from Governmental Accountability Office criticism, but also from a degree of frustration with the internal Air Force perception of their own space "operators", the divergent interpretation of the use of the term "operator" and a requirement to meet ground-based needs with space products that they would not otherwise be able to acquire.

---

[115] Bruce H. McClintock, Major, U.S. Air Force. *The Transformation Trinity.* Air University Press, Maxwell AFB, Alabama. 2002. pp .45-49.

[116] Daniel P. Arthur, Lieutenant Commander, U.S. Navy and Dennis G. Wille, Major, U.S. Army. *"A Proposed Architecture for Theater Coordination of Global Space Capabilities."* Naval Postgraduate School Thesis, Monterey, CA. 2006. pp. 35-41.

1. **Government Accountability Office and the Executive Agent for Space**

These differences are highlighted in the 2004 GAO report. It focuses on implementation failings in the DoD Space Human Capital Resources Strategy, both at the DoD, as well as individual service levels. The strategy, as published, contained strategic goals and objectives, but did not contain an implementation plan with specific actions, timeframes and goals. The timeframe and release of the DoD Space Human Capital Resources Strategy and the 2004 GAO report bear a close relationship, and examination of the timing and recommendations resemble a ping-pong match:

- Service: February 2004 – DoD Executive Agent for Space releases DoD Space Human Capital Resources Strategy.
- Volley: August 2004 – Government Accountability Office releases report on DoD Space Human Capital Resources Strategy.
- Volley: December 2004 – DoD Executive Agent for Space releases DoD Space Human Capital Resources Implementation Strategy.

The Executive Agent for Space managed to release its Space Human Capital Resources Implementation plan before the close of 2004 - an exceptionally quick response for a policy and doctrine publication. Clearly, the criticisms in the 2004 GAO report were considered valid, important and addressable by the Executive Agent for Space.

The rapid response to the GAO report on the part of the Secretary of the Air Force is indicative of the seriousness which that service (Air Force) approaches space planning and policy. Indeed, the 2004 GAO report is as, if not more, critical of shortcomings in U.S. Navy and Army implementation of Space Cadre planning and execution as it is of the Department of Defense as a whole.

2. **The Good…**

For comparison, by August 2004, the Air Force had an approved strategic Space Cadre plan with delineated implementation objectives, and was in the neighborhood of completing 90% of their goals – to include:

- Identification of all of the personnel making up the cadre (more than 10,000 members at that time).

59

- Development and implementation of an education and training program, as well as a progression plan professional development.
- Identification and definition of Space Cadre positions along with certification and educational requirements for those jobs.
- Identification of financial resources for implementation of Space Cadre initiatives.
- Designation of a certification program for personnel.
- Establishment of a permanent space professional management function.[117]

Similarly, the Marine Corps evidenced a clear institutional understanding of their needs for space-savvy professionals, and the 2004 GAO report details the Marine strategy which includes the following list of ten objectives for developing space professionals:

- Establish an identifiable cadre of space-qualified enlisted and civilian marines.
- Create and staff additional space personnel positions in the operating forces.
- Create and staff additional space positions at national security space organizations.
- Improve space operations professional military education for all Marine Corps officers.
- Focus the graduate education of Marine Corps space operations students to support Marine Corps needs
- Leverage inter-service space training to ensure the development and proficiency of the space cadre
- Develop a management process through which interested officers can be assigned to multiple space-related positions during their careers and still compete for promotion with their peers.
- Develop a process and structure for space professionals in the Marine Corps reserves through which they can support operations, training, and exercises through augmentation and mobilization
- Fully participate in the DoD Executive Agent for Space's efforts to create a space cadre
- Incorporate appropriate space professional certification processes into the management of the Marine Corps' space cadre.[118]

---

[117] United States. *Report to Congressional Committees: Defense Space Activities: Additional Actions Needed to Implement Human Capital Strategy and Develop Space Personnel.* Government Accountability Office. August 2004. pp. 13-14. http://www.gao.gov/new.itmes/d04697.pdf. June 2007.

The Air Force and the Marine Corps could not be more different in their approach to space systems, effects and utilization. The Air Force identifies space as a core competency of the service in general,[119] and is responsible for the full spectrum of space-related endeavors, from engineering design and construction of space systems, to the full spectrum of strategic, operational and tactical utilization of those assets. DoD membership in the Air Force Space Cadre currently numbers 7,434, both officer and enlisted ranks. The Marine Corps, by contrast, has a space cadre membership of only 110 active and reserve members (as of September 2005), whose mission it is to provide Marine Corps representation in the requirements definition process for acquisition of space systems, and to leverage space systems in support of Marine Corps missions.[120] Though startlingly different in scope and service philosophy, the Air Force and Marine Corps' share a critical commonality in their construction of Space Cadres and the composition of their Space Cadre Human Capital Strategies. These two institutions have a clear understanding of the capabilities, roles and requirements of space systems in their respective warfare areas. As a result, they exhibit a fundamental comprehension of what roles they expect their personnel to execute in the management and operation of space-related capabilities, and they plan, staff and spend accordingly.

3. ...the Bad...

In marked contrast to the clear and unobstructed view of the Air Force and Marine Corps with respect to their Space Cadres', the Navy of 2004 was navigating through thick fog, uncertain of where its Space Cadre was destined, much less the roles, missions and tasks required to reach a destination. The document governing Navy Space Cadre efforts

---

[118] United States. *Report to Congressional Committees: Defense Space Activities: Additional Actions Needed to Implement Human Capital Strategy and Develop Space Personnel.* Government Accountability Office. August 2004. pp. 15-16. http://www.gao.gov/new.itmes/d04697.pdf. June 2007.

[119] United States. Joint Publication 3-33, *Joint Force Capabilities.* Department of Defense. 13 October 1999. pp. vi-vii.

[120] United States. *Statement of Brigadier General Thomas A. Benes, Director, Strategy and Plans Division. Plans, Policies, and Operation Department. Headquarters, United States Marine Corps.* House Armed Services Committee. Space Budget Activities. 9 March 2005. p. 3.
<http://www.globalsecurity.org/space/library/congress/2005_h/050309-benes.pdf>. June 2007.
"...leverage warfighting capabilities in Space and Global Strike, Intelligence, Surveillance, and Reconnaissance (ISR), Integrated Missile Defense (IMD), and Information Operations."

at that time was a Secretary of the Navy Instruction, SECNAVINST 5400.39C, Department of the Navy Space Policy, released 6 April 2004. This instruction, reflecting the criticism of the 2004 GAO report, contains only policy generalities and platitudes on the subjects of Sea Power 21,[121] the National Security Space organization, and inter-agency relations. It failed to identify critical space billets, required numbers of space personnel, performance measures, required resources and a central organizational manager for the community.

The Army suffered similar criticism in the 2004 GAO report, with gaps identified in centralization of management functions for their cadre, lack of critical billet definition, and identification of civilian and enlisted personnel as Space Cadre members. The Army however, had established a specific and tangible career path for space operations officers, education and training requirements for the same, and had studies underway to identify the proper numbers of these personnel and the billets with the highest fill requirements. As of the summer of 2007, the Army has completed identification of their space cadre personnel and required positions, had has studies ongoing to refine training needs, job-task analysis and continues to perform data collection and tracking.[122]

4. ...and the Ugly

Although not specifically branded by the Government Accountability Office as the DoD component with the most lackluster space-qualified personnel management system, one of the implications of the 2004 GAO report was that the Navy had the farthest to go in developing an effective Space Cadre. Absent any sort of metrics-based space policy, Space Cadre Human Capital Strategy, and concrete, goal based Space Policy, implementation of an effective Navy Space Cadre substantially lagged the other services in meeting the requirements of the DoD Directive 5101.2.

---

[121] Vern Clark, Admiral, U.S. Navy. *Sea Power 21*. Naval Institute Proceedings. October 2002. http://www.navy.mil/navydata/cno/proceedings.html. June 2007.

[122] Army Space Cadre Space Enabler Nomination and Selection Effort (SENSE). 30 January 2007. TRADOC Pam 525-7-4, Army Space Operations Concept Capability Plan (CCP).

C. GROWTH AND MATURATION OF THE NAVY SPACE CADRE.

1. Navy Space Human Capital Strategy

In response to the criticism and recommendations of the August 2004 GAO report, and the evident problems within the Navy space arena, the Department of the Navy stepped up its efforts to more effectively use its Space Human Capital between 2004 and 2007. Following closely on the heels of the GAO report, in December of 2004, the Navy issued its Navy Space Cadre Human Capital Strategy. This document, while lacking the clarity of (for example) the Marine Corps Space Strategy, expands greatly upon the Department of the Navy Space Policy (SECNAVINST 5400.39C), establishing specific missions and purposes for the Cadre as a whole, identifying membership and makeup of the Navy Space Cadre, specifying membership requirements, limited personnel tracking mechanisms and approximate size, delineating roles and responsibilities for selected Space Cadre leadership positions, and stating specific goals for the strategy. Perhaps most importantly, the Navy Space Cadre Human Capital Strategy clearly identifies the tasks inherent in the following space/space cadre-related positions:

- Functional Authority (Commander, Naval Network Warfare Command)
- Space Cadre Advisor
- Assistant Space Cadre Advisor

Centralization of organization and planning for the Navy Space Cadre, an issue identified as a major topic heading in the August 2004 GAO report,[123] achieved an obvious high priority in the Navy's space professional efforts. Appointment of Commander, Naval Network Warfare Command (NNWC) as the Space Cadre Functional Authority effectively ties the implementation of Navy Space Cadre policy and Human

---

[123] United States. *Report to Congressional Committees: Defense Space Activities: Additional Actions Needed to Implement Human Capital Strategy and Develop Space Personnel.* Government Accountability Office. August 2004. p. 18. http://www.gao.gov/new.itmes/d04697.pdf. June 2007. Topic heading reads specifically "Navy Has Initiated Steps in Developing Its Space Cadre, but It Has No Strategy or Focal Point."

Capital Strategy to operational requirements at the network, Fleet, and Joint levels.[124] Moreover, as the heir to the disestablished Naval Space Command, NETWARCOM is the natural functional authority for the "virtual community"[125] of Navy Space Cadre personnel.

2. Navy Space Cadre Advisor

Identification and selection of the Navy Space Cadre Advisor and the newer Assistant Space Cadre Advisor are evidenced as essential from the standpoint of Navy leadership. To date, all three of the Naval officers that have served as the Space Cadre Advisor have been high-profile, highly-educated, proven performers who brought ambition and drive to the otherwise stagnant Navy efforts at codifying the requirements and responsibilities of the Navy Space Cadre. Composition of the Navy Space Cadre Human Capital Strategy, analysis and enunciation of Navy Space officer billets, construction of a notional career path, integration of reserve officer space experts, identification of Civil Service Component space experts, development of the NNWC MOC Space Cell and development of proposed training pipelines have all occurred between 2004 and 2007. Additionally, fit and fill rates (metrics to identify personnel placed in a job for which they have appropriate training, and to identify the percentage of the total number of Navy Space jobs filled, respectively) for Navy Space Cadre personnel have climbed significantly since the codification of the Navy Space Human Capital Strategy (for a representative Operations-specific example, see Figure 6, below).

---

[124] Department of the Navy. OPNAVINST 5400.43A, *Navy Space Policy Implementation*. 12 February 2007. pp. 7-8.
https://doni.daps.dla.mil/Directives/Forms/AllItems.aspx?RootFolder=%2fDirectives%2f05000%20General%20Management%20Security%20and%20Safety%20Services%2f05%2d400%20Organization%20and%20Functional%20Support%20Services. May 2007.

[125] Department of the Navy. OPNAVINST 5400.43A, *Navy Space Policy Implementation*. 12 February 2007. p. 3.
https://doni.daps.dla.mil/Directives/Forms/AllItems.aspx?RootFolder=%2fDirectives%2f05000%20General%20Management%20Security%20and%20Safety%20Services%2f05%2d400%20Organization%20and%20Functional%20Support%20Services. May 2007.

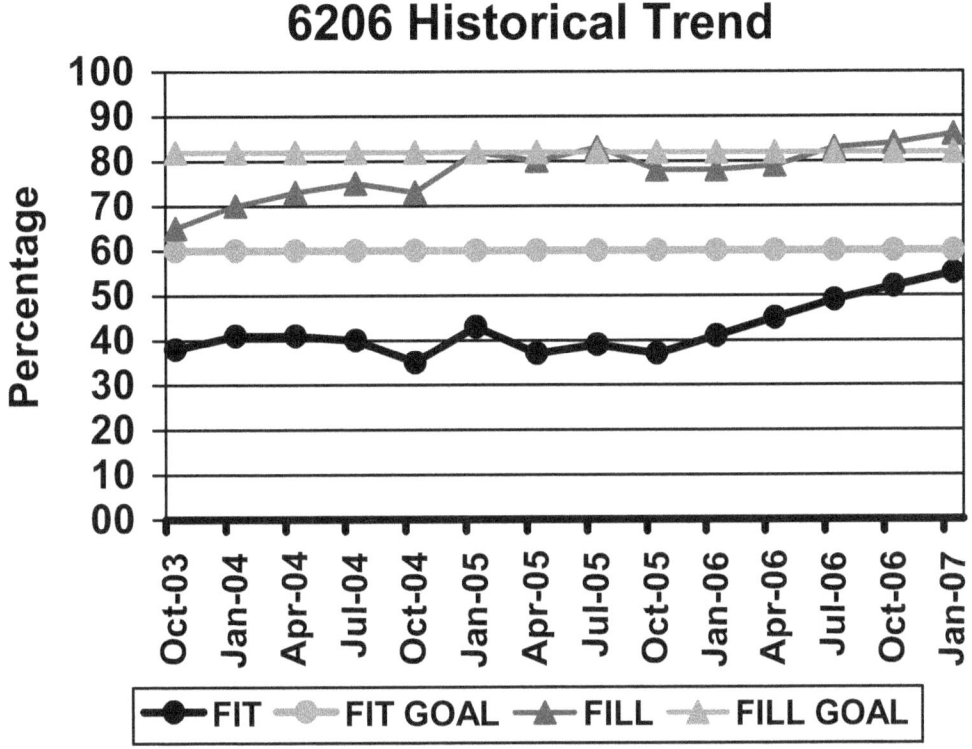

Figure 6.   Space Systems Operations Subspecialty Historical Fit and Fill Rates.[126]

3. Shortfalls

The Navy Space Cadre Human Capital Strategy does not, however, address the following issues – issues of great import when viewed against the background of the fully established, mission-oriented Space Cadre of the Air Force, and the revised 2006 National Space Policy:

- Articulation of required Core Competencies for Navy Space personnel.
- Composition of a list of "Best Practices" for the Navy Space community.
- Establishment of a list of billets critical to the Navy Space community.
- Construction and validation of a Navy Space Cadre Professional Certification.

---

[126] Julie Niedermaier, Commander, U.S. Navy. *Navy Space Cadre Update (SSFA Space Indoctrination)*. PowerPoint Brief. March 2007. Slide 6.

- Integration of enlisted space experts within the service into the Navy Space Cadre.

- Proposal of a notional "virtual" career progression for the various parent communities hosting Space Cadre members.

- Description of a career-long training program to establish a baseline knowledge requirement for Space Cadre personnel.

- Clarification of the relationship between the "virtual community manager"[127] of the Navy Space Cadre and the formalized parent community detailers for Space Cadre members.

- Management of, or input to the promotion of Space Cadre personnel for the purpose of maintaining an educated senior leadership in the community.

- Validation of the above measures by senior Navy leadership.

All of these measures are shortfalls noted within the Navy Space Human Capital Strategy, identifying them as clearly within the radar horizon of the community leadership, but beyond the sensor range of senior Navy leadership. Additionally, these shortfalls in the Navy's strategy are notable in that they have all been solved by other services. For example, Air Force and Army Human Capital Strategies have progressed to the point where the Air Force has developed a training program at the National Security Space Institute[128] that fills joint requirements for space training and, as of 2005, supported a student population that was disproportionately comprised of services other than the Air Force.[129] The Army uses a three-level certification program for its space professionals that was designed by and for the Air Force, and even recognizes the award of the Air Force qualification badges for wear on Army uniforms. Career progression, critical-fill jobs, core competencies and full manpower integration are clearly solvable

---

[127] The term "virtual community manager" appears on OPNAVINST 5400.43A, 12 Feb 07, page 3. It is used in the sense of a collaborative group of individuals from disparate backgrounds and warfighting specialties working towards a common, overarching goal. Specifically, the "virtual community manager" has no authority to assign personnel to billets, only to provide representation and exposure for the Navy Space Cadre to fill assignments that have been established as within the field of Navy Space. The concept is also an intrinsic component of the "cross-designator community."

[128] Located in Colorado Springs, CO, previously the Air Force Space Operations School.

[129] 2005 NSSI composition breakdown was 79% USAF, 21% Other. This is in contrast to the total number of space positions in the DoD – 94% USAF, 6% Other. United States. *Report to Congressional Committees: Defense Space Activities: Management Guidance and Performance Measures Needed to Develop Personnel.* Government Accountability Office. September 2005. pp. 19-21. http://www.gao.gov/cgi-bin/getrep?GAO-05-833. June 2007.

problems. The shortfalls or gaps in the Navy Space Cadre Human Capital Strategy result more from high-level leadership dysfunction and lack of understanding than inability on the part of the Space Cadre to solve them.

Indeed, the mention of other services' solutions to implementing the requirements of Department of Defense Directives brings to the fore a broad-scope question - *If other services have accepted the notion of joint training and education, core competencies, career requirements, and common certifications, why has the Navy not acknowledged these solutions?*

D. CONTINUANCE AND PROMOTION OF THE NAVY SPACE CADRE

1. Promotion Board Precept Language

As one facet of the effort to ensure broad distribution of space proficiency throughout the fleet, and to enhance representation of the Navy Space Cadre at more senior levels, officer promotion boards since 2003 have included language that highlights the need to promote and retain personnel with space education and experience.[130] Promotion and retention of Navy personnel with extensive space training is critically important to the future of the Navy Space Cadre, as fluctuations in the promotion rates or perception of "glass ceilings" for community members has the potential to detract from future space cadre membership. The text of the message to the promotion boards is included below:

> PRECEPT LANGUAGE FROM FY07 AD 04/05/06 LINE BOARDS
>
> Success of naval operations is dependent on the capabilities of national, DoD and commercial space support. It is imperative that the Navy develops a significant cadre, comprised of the URL and RL communities, that is competent in relating the areas of operations, requirements, development and acquisition to space. Members of this cadre may have atypical career paths because of specialized education, training and assignments outside of the Navy. This cadre will continue to represent the Navy in mid-level and senior joint billets, as well as be assigned to Navy billets in direct support of space requirements and acquisition. When selecting the best and fully qualified officers to meet the needs of the

---

[130] Department of the Navy. *Navy Space Cadre Human Capital Strategy.* 27 December 2004. p. 16.

Navy, you must view the quality of performance of offices in the Space Cadre as having weight equal to that ordinarily given to the quality of performance of other members of their respective communities who have followed more traditional career paths.[131]

This effort has evidently borne fruit, as the promotion rates for O-5 and O-6 Space Cadre members has been generally slightly higher than rates for their contemporaries without the Space Cadre subspecialty. (See Figure 7, below.)

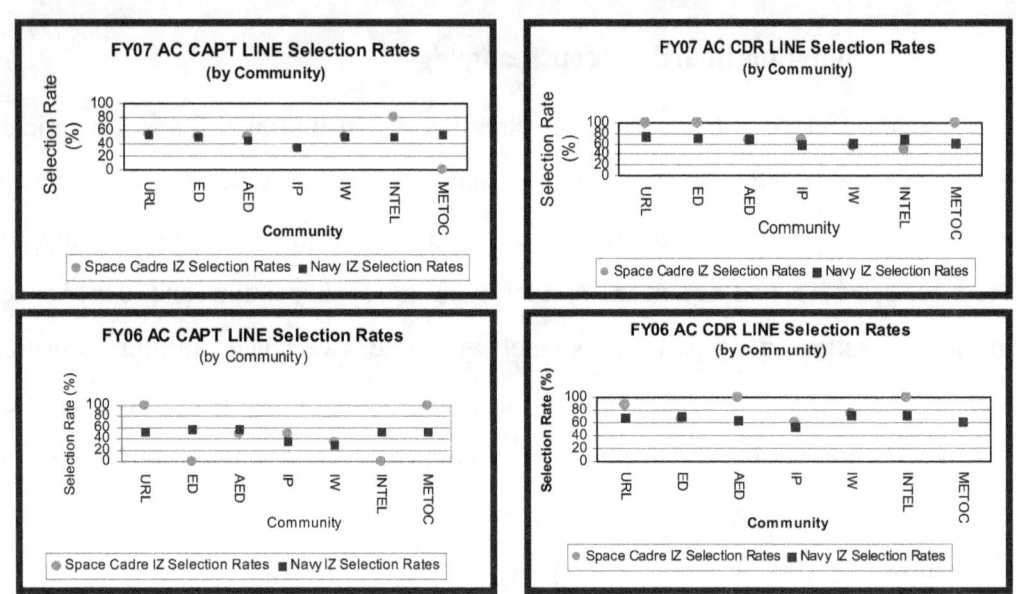

Figure 7. In-Zone Promotion Rates for Navy Space Cadre Personnel.[132]

2. Additional Qualification Designations and Subspecialty Codes

In an effort to codify the accomplishments of Space Cadre personnel within the community and present this information to promotion boards, a four-level Additional

---

[131] Julie Niedermaier, Commander, U.S. Navy. *Navy Space Cadre Update (SSFA Space Indoctrination)*. PowerPoint Brief. March 2007. Slide 25 Notes.

[132] Ibid., Slide 25 Notes.

Qualification Designator (AQD) scheme was introduced following the 2003 promotion board. The four levels are as follows:

- VS1 – Recruit: Requires only Space Certificate, no experience
- VS2 – Apprentice: Requires space-related undergraduate degree or 18 months of experience in a space billet
- VS3 – Journeyman: Requires space-related undergraduate degree plus 18 months of experience or space-related masters' degree or 36+ months of experience.
- VS4 – Expert: Requires space-related masters' degree plus 18 months of experience or space-related PhD or 10 years of experience.

Although these AQD codes are in place in the Navy personnel system and Officer Service Records, it is unclear as to whether the addition of these codes is sufficient to identify exceptionally qualified Space Cadre personnel for promotion. The Navy Space Cadre Human Capital Strategy specifically identifies this as a topic requiring assessment.[133]

Confusion in the qualification process and identification of Navy space personnel stems in part from the labeling system. AQDs may be earned through either certificate programs or experience. Subspecialty Codes may also be earned through experience or formal education. Either a Subspecialty Code or an AQD is required for assignment to a Space-coded billet, but completion of a space-coded job is necessary for the award of some AQDs and Subspecialty Codes. The two Subspecialty Codes are 5500 (Space Systems Engineering) and 6206 (Space Systems Operations). Officer billets in Navy space are identified by these two codes, and as of 2007, there were 315 of these positions available, primarily in the 6206 specialty. Officers with Space Cadre Subspecialty Codes are further differentiated through the use of a suffix to the four-digit code, "T" for officers currently enrolled in a Space Systems educational curricula, "P" for officers who have completed educational requirements for the code, but have not yet served in a space-coded billet, "S/R" for Subspecialty Codes awarded on the basis of experience, and "N/Q" for officers with who have both an approved Space Systems degree and have filled a space-coded billet. Clearly, the system could use some refinement and clarification.

---

[133] Department of the Navy. *Navy Space Cadre Human Capital Strategy.* 27 December 2004. p. 16.

E. CURRENT SPACE CADRE PERSONNEL ASSIGNMENT EFFORTS

Of the 315 Navy Space Cadre Billets, 70 are at-sea billets and 208 are Joint billets. This apparent skew toward ashore positions (approximately 78%) itself poses a problem for the credibility of the Space Cadre with seagoing "warfighter" communities. In an era of increasingly lean budgets and support to expeditionary warfare missions, the Navy perceives potential for cost savings and efficiency gains in personnel assignment by eliminating shore-based jobs in favor of manning positions aboard ships and in the Arabian Gulf region.

1. The Sea – Shore Rotation Conundrum

The threat posed by potential elimination of Navy presence in shore billets, and especially joint shore billets, cannot be overstated. As the Navy influence in space systems and operations has waned, the Space Cadre personnel filling positions where they have ready contact with members of the greater DoD space community are the only remaining leverage that the Navy has to apply to fulfill needs supported by space systems. Without input provided by operational, military Navy space personnel, Navy needs for space systems will be unfilled, as the requirements and acquisition process for these systems proceeds.

On the flip-side of the coin, officers positioned in space billets must have a close and abiding connection with operational Navy forces. The default position of the existing Navy Space community leadership is that this connection to Fleet operations must be accomplished through at-sea, operational experience.[134] The current Navy Space Cadre Advisor states:

> In order to foster an understanding of Space Operations within the Fleet, it is essential for Space-qualified officers to return to the fleet, where they can utilize their knowledge. Likewise, the Space community relies on

---

[134] Victor See, Rear Admiral, U.S. Navy. *CHIPS Interview.* CHIPS. January 2006. http://www.chips.navy.mil/archives/06_Jan/web_pages/RADM_SEE.htm. June 2007.

these personnel to come up with innovative solutions to warfighting gaps. To accomplish this, Space Cadre officers must have significant operational experience.[135]

Plainly, it is desirable for Space Cadre personnel assigned to operational and seagoing units to possess a degree of expertise in space systems and operations. From the standpoint of the formally educated Navy Space Cadre members, use of the degree provided by the Naval Postgraduate School is largely wasted. Amongst the graduates of the 2002 to 2007 Space Systems Operations curricula, only 21% of Navy officers were assigned to a space-coded billet immediately after graduation. The achievement of a masters' degree is of great potential value to the Navy, but attainment of true space expertise cannot occur exclusively in an educational setting. Experience and interaction with members of the greater DoD space community in the fielding and operation of satellite systems is necessary to ripen the fruits of formal education. Further, the space systems that the Navy depends upon for communication, navigation, surveillance, and forecasting are largely acquired and operated by other services – without joint interaction prior to Navy-specific operations, Navy Space Cadre members will have an inadequate understanding of the capabilities and limitations of the systems and effects they will be expected to provide. The resulting uphill battle in attempting to provide commanders with the information, capabilities and services they desire at the operational level will prove a frustration to both commanders and operators alike. Worse, the lack of functional expertise and resulting weak job performance will diminish the credibility of the Space Cadre as a whole, exacerbating the problem of leadership ambivalence with regard to space-provided capabilities.

2. Seagoing Space Cadre Support and the CSG-8 Space Team

In the current Navy environment, application of space knowledge at the operational level is very much in its infancy. Though billets requiring space Subspecialty Codes and AQDs are being established at seagoing staff and large-deck shipboard levels, realization of the capabilities and proficiencies that are *supposed* to be

---

[135] Julie Niedermaier, Commander, U.S. Navy. *Navy Space Cadre Update (SSFA Space Indoctrination)*. PowerPoint Brief. March 2007. Slide 8 Notes.

innate to Space Cadre members lags the personnel management paperwork. The primary reason for the gap between the on-paper requirement for space know-how afloat and the actual implementation of that know-how is the fact that the space jobs are, without exception, collateral duties shipboard. Herein lies another major shortcoming with the "cross-designator community" concept of the Navy Space Cadre. In the typical shipboard environment, the officer's focus of effort must be on their primary duty. Collateral duties, by nature, are secondary to the primary job assignment. For this reason, space subspecialty coding for particular billets at sea is generally a paper tiger, with only as much bite as an individual has spare time to focus on that secondary mission.

A notable exception to this de-facto standard is the rollout of the Naval Space Campaign and concept implementation of the Carrier Strike Group 8 (CSG-8), Fleet Executive Agent for Space deployment. While the staff manning and structure for the Carrier Strike Group 8 Staff (embarked in USS Dwight D. Eisenhower, CVN-69) remained unchanged from the standard embarked staff, CSG-8 was selected to receive a very robust series of space-related training and education courses, site visits to space support and effects providers (primarily national systems/organizations), and extensive information/capabilities training for the Strike Group Commander.[136] This "space superuser" staff was chartered as a portion of the Naval Space Campaign Plan to validate the following objectives:

- Develop Maritime-specific Space Requirements: Develop space requirements based on current capabilities and limitations of space systems.

- Satisfy Maritime Requirements: Ensure space systems provided by the Executive Agent (EA) for Space and National Security Space sector provide desired effects to meet maritime requirements, and provide feedback through the Naval Capabilities Development Process if they do not.

- Increase Space Knowledge: Promote a better understanding in the fleet of how space-provided effects support maritime operations and scheme of maneuver.

---

[136] Zigmond Leszcynski, Commander, U.S. Navy. *NNWC Space Training, Education, Cadre Turnover. PowerPoint Brief.* Carrier Strike Group 8. March 2005.

- Improve Combat Effectiveness: Improve fleet combat effectiveness with smarter, more aggressive use of space-based capabilities, focusing on maximizing effects for the Carrier Strike Group (CSG) and Expeditionary Strike Group (ESG).

- Improve Human Capital: Cultivate Navy Space Cadre expertise for assignment into joint space and National Security Space (NSS) billets.

- Ingrain Cultural Change: Harvest space-related best practices from Naval Space Campaign lessons learned and institutionalize them through doctrine and policy.

- Understand Space System Vulnerabilities: Ensure Navy seniors understand the vulnerabilities of space systems and mitigation options.[137]

The recognition and success that the CSG-8 experiment achieved can be traced to the uncommon efforts of one individual on that staff. In much the same way as recent refinement and development of the Navy Space Cadre can be traced to the current Space Cadre Advisor, the CSG-8 Air Operations Officer, a Space Cadre member functioned as the Deputy, Space Warfare Commander to the Commander, Carrier Strike Group 8. The status of this position, a collateral duty as noted above, was significantly elevated for the purpose of the Naval Space Campaign effort, yet the officer assigned to the position continued to perform both his "warfare specialty" job as a primary assignment and his Space Cadre job at superlative levels. Apparent boundless energy was evidenced in the production of daily space-effects briefs and leadership of a space planning team between 2004 and 2007. Presence of this high level of commitment to exercise of available space resources and leadership attention to the capabilities inherent in space-enabling the staff led directly to improved situational awareness on the part of the Strike Group Commander.

Unfortunately, this level of commitment and energy, while desirable, is not sufficiently pervasive in any community, or sustainable for an individual. The space after-action report from CSG-8's deployment specifically recommends not only continuation of the training program for deployed staffs, but also that...

> ...the Navy support establishment of Space Operations Officers in Strike Groups and MOCs (Maritime Operations Centers) to ensure close

---
[137] Department of the Navy. *Naval Space Campaign Plan, 2005-2007.* pp. 4, 8. 13 November 2005.

coordination with the Theater Space Coordinating Authority and consistency of Navy space operations in theater.[138]

Validation of the premise that a dedicated Space Operations officer should be assigned to Strike Group Staffs may be a foregone conclusion when considering that the experiment was chartered by the Navy Space Campaign. That the recommendation is internally consistent with the Navy Space Cadre Human Capital Strategy does not, however, invalidate it – one of the stated goals of the Strategy is to "Gain senior leadership support throughout the Navy",[139] and that leadership support can come only with a point of focus within the operational staff that simultaneously provides space effects and can promote the cause of the Navy Space Cadre.

3. Navy Space Cadre in the Joint and National Environment

As a result of the efforts of the Navy Space Cadre leadership between 2004 and 2007, the community has grown substantially in numbers, potential billets and influence. As of February 2007, the Navy Space Cadre numbered approximately 1500 personnel, grouped as follows:

- 780 Active Duty Officer
- 100 Reserve Officer
- 140 Civil Service Civilian
- 500 Enlisted (not yet fully integrated into Navy Space Cadre).[140]

This population is up from 511 personnel identified for the September 2005 GAO report.

The growth in the Navy Space Cadre, or more properly, identification of personnel with the required skill-set to qualify for Space Cadre membership, contrasts most vividly with Air Force membership. By 2005, the Air Force had essentially completed identification of their Space Cadre personnel, and reported 7,434 personnel,

---

[138] Zigmond Leszczynski, Commander, U.S. Navy. *EISENHOWER Strike Group End-Of-Deployment Report, Space Segment*. Carrier Strike Group 8. May 2007.

[139] Department of the Navy. *Navy Space Cadre Human Capital Strategy*. 27 December 2004. p. 16.

[140] Julie Niedermaier, Commander, U.S. Navy. *Navy Space Cadre Update (SSFA Space Indoctrination)*. PowerPoint Brief. March 2007. Slide 8 Notes.

comprised of 6,051 Officers and 1,383 Enlisted. This almost order-of-magnitude difference in Cadre size is only the tip of the iceberg. The Air Force identifies 7,195 space positions for their personnel base, representing a 97% utilization rate for their Space Cadre.[141] The Army has a similar utilization rate for its Space Cadre. In contrast, because of the "cross-community" nature of the Navy Space Cadre, more than half of Navy officers with space training and qualifications are employed in jobs that are unrelated to space and have *no* requirement for the training these personnel possess. Across the DoD, only 315 positions for Navy Officer Space Cadre members exist, providing a 40% utilization rate for this community. This gross mismatch of availability of space-trained personnel with the number of space-related jobs under Navy control is a necessity under the current Navy Space Cadre "cross community" construct, but represents a waste of training, education and manpower resources when those personnel are employed outside of space-related billets.

Additionally, because of the allocation of funding and resources for space within the DoD, Navy Space Cadre are under-represented within their own service. 66% of positions available to Navy Space Cadre are located within the Joint arena, outside of the Navy organization.[142] With approximately 93% of the entire DoD budget for space under their purview,[143] the Air Force "owns", or has the primary historical tie to most of the Joint commands that manage DoD space.[144]

In combination with service dominance of military space efforts, extensive Air Force education, training, certification, policy and doctrine, and personnel management

---

[141] United States. *Report to Congressional Committees: Defense Space Activities: Management Guidance and Performance Measures Needed to Develop Personnel.* Government Accountability Office. September 2005. pp. 18-19. http://www.gao.gov/cgi-bin/getrep?GAO-05-833. June 2007.

[142] United States. *Report to Congressional Committees: Defense Space Activities: Management Guidance and Performance Measures Needed to Develop Personnel.* Government Accountability Office. September 2005. p. 19. http://www.gao.gov/cgi-bin/getrep?GAO-05-833. June 2007.

Julie Niedermaier, Commander, U.S. Navy. *Navy Space Cadre Update (SSFA Space Indoctrination).* PowerPoint Brief. March 2007. Slide 7.

[143] United States. *Report to Congressional Committees: Defense Space Activities: Management Guidance and Performance Measures Needed to Develop Personnel.* Government Accountability Office. September 2005. p. 7. http://www.gao.gov/cgi-bin/getrep?GAO-05-833. June 2007.

[144] To wit: U.S. Strategic Command, National Reconnaissance Office, Joint Space Operations Center, Cheyenne Mountain, Northern Command.

systems already in place have the potential to provide a sound structure for Navy Space Cadre formalization efforts . Navy acceptance and officially sanctioned use of some of the methods and systems in place in the Air Force not only could contribute to the cause of enhancing jointness, but also reduce redundancies in planning, execution and management of the service-specific Space Cadre. As an example, Army acceptance of Air Force training and certification as part of their Space Cadre professional development is an outstanding example of simplicity and synergy. Use of National Security Space Institute education and Certified Space Professional standards supply the Army with a method for meeting DoD Space Cadre requirements, and neatly centralizes the expertise required to produce space-smart personnel. Further, accepting the established Air Force solutions with respect to personnel eliminates non-core-competency tasks from the Army's slate. In an era of declining budgets and business-outsourcing, strategic integration of service efforts in maintaining and furthering their Space Cadres is viable option.

For the Navy, specifically, full development and utilization of experts in space systems and operations is a necessity. Though direct Navy involvement in the business of space has waned, reliance on the services and products provided by space systems continues to grow. Operators, managers and leadership throughout the Navy need to be supported by a community of space experts. Further, the time and commitment required to acquire and implement that know-how must not be detrimental to promotion of those experts. The current trend of growing recognition of these facts must be nurtured, and funded commensurate with the field's importance to Navy operations in a asymmetric, networked combat environment. The evidence clearly indicates that highly trained personnel with substantial space expertise placed in positions where they can affect leverage on national space efforts promote the cause of the Navy Space Cadre, Navy Space Campaign, Sea Power 21 and the national interest.

V. NAVY SPACE: CORE BUSINESSES AND OUTSOURCING

Institutional inertia and organizational culture can represent reasons why bureaucracies behave in certain ways, but do not necessarily validate methods and practices.[145] With an established and valued history in the space arena, persistence and maintenance of a corporate "space culture" is a source of pride to the Navy. Additionally the Navy and its space community have an established history of scientific and research excellence, and despite recent downturns in the fortunes of Navy space, pockets of that excellence and expertise still exist.

Those few remaining enclaves of "space-smarts" within the Department of the Navy however, are overshadowed by the pulverizing force of a bureaucracy without a clear concept of the intricacies and necessity of space operations or the leadership understanding to implement it.[146] Benign neglect and relegation of space to the status of a non-critical supporting function have threatened the last remnants of the Navy's tradition of space excellence. Without a steering force applied to the institution and a re-assessment of what space missions are of critical value to the Navy, the remaining corporate knowledge inherent in the Navy's scattered space organizations and nascent Space Cadre is likely to fragment and disappear entirely.

This chapter will focus on the Navy's existing space systems operation, space support to operational forces, and acquisition programs. Emphasis on the organizations that perform those missions and the relative validity of current focus of effort and structure will be examined. Present Navy use of and requirements for space will be considered, and alternatives for achieving those aims discussed.

---

[145] James Q. Wilson. *Bureaucracy: What Government Agencies Do and Why They Do It.* Chapter 6, Various. 1989.

[146] United States. *Transcript of House Armed Services Committee Hearing No. 108–40, Hearing on Space Cadre/Space Professionals.* House of Representatives. One Hundred Eighth Congress, Second Session. 22 July 2004. http://commdocs.house.gov/committees/security/has204290.000/has204290_0f.htm. June 2007.

A.   REDUNDANCY IN THE REALM OF CONTROL

The current Department of Defense construct for flying communications satellites defies description.[147] Like other functions that are a result of historical legacy, methods for command and control of satellite systems are as convoluted and scattered as the flight of an inebriated butterfly.[148] Operation of the various components of a single orbital object may be conducted by multiple agencies, with only minimal coordination amongst the parties involved. Worse, the vast majority of the personnel, funding and facilities used for satellite operation belong to the Air Force, but only very rarely is the Air Force the sole stakeholder in satellite resource transactions, or indeed, the sole owner of all of the various subsystems and packages onboard the satellite vehicle. Further, in an attempt to provide satellite services to their deployed forces, the individual armed services perceive a need for service-specific operation of portions of the satellite control segment in order to apply leverage to get the support and products their forces require. As a result, the Army, Navy and Air Force each maintain their own satellite operations commands, infrastructure, and fragmentary space operations missions when it comes to satellite communications.

A much more appropriate business structure to accomplish the missions of satellite operation and control is to consolidate all of these functions under one organization, with appropriate representation from the various service stakeholders. Consolidation can produce cost reductions through the use of shared administration and overhead, and single-entity operation of space systems reduces the internal command complexities inherent in service-specific space operations organizations. As an added benefit, shared service responsibilities for manning a centralized, joint satellite operations

---

[147] Joel Hicks. Commander, U.S. Navy. Email to the authors: *Re: Questions regarding NAVSOC*. 15 June 2007.

[148] In contrast to the convoluted multi-service and agency control of U.S. military satellites, , evolutionary developments in satellite operation and network control within the commercial sector centralize and simplify management tasks through extensive automation. See: AsiaSat (http://suirg.org/press/asiasatpr.pdf), Thruraya, DataPath MaxView (http://www.ilc.com/scheduall_msnbc.html) and IntelSat (http://www.sciatl.com/products/customers/white-papers/originatorwhitepaper.pdf).

and C² organization offers an opportunity for common and cross training of space cadre from all services, and improved stakeholder input to the operations of those systems.

The Air Force, with the lion's share of space-borne assets and tasking has the largest space operations presence, with the 50th Space Wing (50th SW), and their subordinate 50th Space Communications Squadron (50th SCS) involved in the operation of more than 170 Department of Defense satellites.

> The wing operates satellite operation centers at Schriever AFB and remote tracking stations and other command and control facilities around the world. These facilities monitor satellites during launch, put the satellites in their proper orbits following the launch, operate the satellites while they are in orbit and keep them functioning properly.[149]

More specifically, the 50th Space Communications Squadron claims the following mission areas:

> 50th SCS executes command and control functions supporting $50 billion in national satellite and terrestrial systems for the President, United States of America, allied and coalition forces. The squadron operates and maintains communications-computer systems establishing real-time global connectivity to more than 170 satellites comprising the Global Positioning System, Defense Meteorological Satellite Program, Defense Satellite Program, Defense Satellite Communications System, Milstar, Fleet Satellite Communications System, Ultra High Frequency Follow-On System, North Atlantic Treaty Organization, Defense Advanced Research Program Agency and test system satellites through the $8.2 billion Air Force Satellite Control Network.[150]

With some evident overlap in claimed mission area with the 50th Space Communications Squadron, the Naval Satellite Operations Center asserts the following missions:

- UHF Follow-On (*UFO*) satellite constellation that provides the military UHF narrow-band voice and data communications.

- Polar satellite that is equipped with an Enhanced EHF (EEHF) capability.

---

[149] Department of the Air Force. *50th Space Wing Fact Sheet.* Schriever Air Force Base Website. http://www.schriever.af.mil/library/factsheets/factsheet.asp?id=3909. June 2007.

[150] Department of the Air Force. *50th Space Communications Squadron Factsheet.* Schriever Air Force Base Website. http://www.schriever.af.mil/library/factsheets/factsheet.asp?id=3917. June 2007.

- Geodetic Satellite (*GEOSAT*) Follow-On (*GFO*) radar altimeter satellite that provides ocean surface height information to Naval meteorological centers.
- Navy Ionospheric Monitoring System (*NIMS*) satellites, known also as Transit Follow-on (*TFO*) and originally used for global navigation as the precursor to GPS. The four remaining satellites now support upper ionospheric research.
- Mobile Users Objective System (*MUOS*) satellites, a system being developed as a replacement for the *UFO* constellation.[151]

Finally, the Army through its 1st Space Brigade and subordinate 53rd Signal Battalion at Camp Roberts, California,[152] executes the proportionally smallest satellite operations mission, yet again overlapping the claimed Air Force mission:

> The battalion (53rd Signal Battalion) plans and controls the payload of the Defense Satellite Communications System (DSCS) satellites.[153]

These stated assignments fail to adequately define the actual scope of specific operations under a given service's control. The details of satellite system control are convoluted, with operation of the orbital craft partitioned for reasons that stem from engineering design, stand-alone legacy satellite command and control systems and historical basis. The following is an example of the scheme of control, specific to the satellites operated (in part) by the Naval Satellite Operations Center (NAVSOC).

> …NAVSOC controls the bus for *UFO* (which includes the UHF/EHF/EEHF/GBS packages) and will do the same for *MUOS*. NAVSOC also controls the bus for *FLTSAT* (which includes UHF/EHF packages). However, NAVSOC only monitors and commands to the Polar EHF Payload. The bus is on a classified host and we have no visibility into its Health and Status…

> …NAVSOC actually doesn't control the payload in an allocation sense, meaning we do not manage users or control what gets sent from the S/C (spacecraft) or what is sent to the S/C…

---

[151] Department of the Navy. *NAVSOC Mission Statement.* Naval Satellite Operations Center. http://www.nbvc.navy.mil/navsoc/mission.html. June 2007.

[152] Similar operations are conducted by Army units around the world at Fort Detrick, Maryland, Fort Meade, Maryland, Fort Buckner, Japan, and Landsthul, Germany.

[153] Mark Hubbs. *The Eagle.* SMDC/ARSTRAT Historical Office. http://www.smdc.army.mil/Historical/Eagle/Brigades.pdf. June 2007.

> ...NAVSOC's only relationship with the payload is to monitor payload health and status and, when directed, help in troubleshooting by turning transponders on/off or reconfiguring the payload to switch to a redundant mode.[154]

With physical and logical control of the myriad of spacecraft functions, payload functions,[155] and use of the variety of Department of Defense satellites divided functionally, organizationally, geographically, and by specific system interface, there are unquestionable redundancies inherent in the current satellite control construct. While the Air Force is already in control of approximately 93% of the DoD Space Budget,[156] continuation of the status quo (in terms of service-specific satellite operations programs) is senseless. The current satellite control construct exists to provide each service programmatic access to the requirements definition process for new systems and as a historical throwback to the post-World War II era, when independent space programs existed within each of the services. In the modern era of hyper-expensive, long-lead systems and mandatory joint military activity, these legacy motives are no longer valid. To eliminate the redundancies and overhead intrinsic to the fragmented satellite control structure, the Navy should divest itself of the missions performed by NAVSOC and transfer its remaining satellite operation and control responsibilities to the Air Force's 50th Space Wing.

B. NAVY SATELLITE SYSTEMS OPERATIONS

As there is no documented mandate for Navy organizations or personnel to operate satellite systems, limited financial and personnel resources should be targeted to better operational leverage. Policy guidance within the Navy is currently constructed as follows:

---

[154] Joel Hicks. Commander, U.S. Navy. Email to the authors: *Re: Questions regarding NAVSOC*. 15 June 2007.

[155] *exempli gratia:* Resource Allocation, Health and Status of various subsystems, Bus Operation, Launch, Phasing, and stationkeeping

[156] United States. *Report to Congressional Committees: Defense Space Activities: Management Guidance and Performance Measures Needed to Develop Personnel*. Government Accountability Office. September 2005. p. 7. http://www.gao.gov/cgi-bin/getrep?GAO-05-833. June 2007. Figure is specific to then-projected FY 2006 DoD budget for space programs.

> The United States Navy and Marine Corps must maintain their ability to tactically exploit the capabilities provided by space systems and participate in all appropriate aspects of the changed NSS environment in order to function as an integrated member of the Nation's joint warfighting team. Consequently, the DON must continually reassess its approach and investment to ensure that naval forces receive the maximum benefit of space-based capabilities. The DON will: (1) integrate the essential capabilities provided by space systems at every appropriate level throughout the naval force; and (2) shape the outcome of joint deliberations on future space system capabilities to ensure the combat effectiveness of naval forces.[157]

As such, by policy, not just actual practice, the Navy is fulfilling a role in the Department of Defense space arena as a "'ruthless customer' of NSS capabilities."[158] Importance of effects and resources provided by these systems is of primary importance, with minimal consideration given to who the "service provider" is. Whether intentional or not, implementation of this policy by expunging satellite control from the Navy's operational lexicon relieves the Navy and the Network Warfare Command of a peripheral function, and opens the door to other operations for achieving requisite space-based capabilities.

There is little disagreement regarding the proud heritage of the Naval Satellite Operations Center. "...NAVSOC personnel pioneered space system operations when they developed, tested, and implemented the procedures to operate and manage the first operational American space system...."[159] But just as the GPS system closed the book on the world's first satellite navigation system, *TRANSIT,* so the United States Air Force Space Command has engulfed the DoD space world to such a degree that NAVSOC's efforts are increasingly marginalized. In-house NAVSOC efforts in commanding and controlling satellites have devolved to a 146-person effort for the Point Mugu, California

---

[157] Department of the Navy. SECNAV Instruction 5400.39C: *Department of Navy Space Policy*. 6 April 2004. Section 4.. http://ftp.fas.org/irp/doddir/navy/secnavinst/5400_39c.pdf. June 2007.

[158] National Research Council. Committee on the Navy's Needs in Space for Providing Future Capabilities. *The Navy's Needs in Space for Providing Future Capabilities*. The National Academies Press 2005. Executive Summary, p. 4. http://books.nap.edu/openbook.php?record_id=11200&page=4. June 2007.

[159] Naval Satellite Operations Center. *Modern Satellite Operations, NAVSOC Fact Sheet*. http://www.nbvc.navy.mil/navsoc/docs/FactSheet.pdf. Quote is specifically in reference to the *TRANSIT* satellite-based navigation system.

organization.[160] Once a manpower-intensive, 24-hour-a-day operation, automation and mission reduction have relieved requirements for personnel, and NAVSOC efforts are very limited in scope, with only 23 satellites under mostly contractor control[161] as of early 2006.[162]

Elimination of the Navy component of the satellite command and control function is an almost trivial undertaking, and can assist in a tidy centralization of satellite operation efforts. The equipment, infrastructure and operational presence required to fly and operate the NAVSOC satellite inventory already exists at the Air Force's 14th Air Force and subordinate 50th Space Wing. Additionally, from an organizational structure standpoint, NAVSOC currently falls under the tactical control (TACON) of the Joint Space Operations Center (JSpOC), another organization subordinate to Commander, 14th Air Force. Years of command cooperation and careful definition and nurturing of command relationships could allow for the addition of Navy representation at the 50th Space Wing and 14th Air Force to ensure Navy requirements previously met by the NAVSOC are met. Providentially, NAVSOC Detachment DELTA is located at Schriever AFB and currently serves as the alternate Satellite Operations Center to the Point Mugu Headquarters.[163] This proposed merger is supported by existing facilities and command relationships.

---

[160] Paul M. Insch, Captain, U.S. Navy. *NAVSOC Command Brief.* Naval Satellite Operations Center. PowerPoint Brief. June 2006. Slide 12.

[161] Joel Hicks. Commander, U.S. Navy. Email to the authors: *Re: Questions regarding NAVSOC.* 15 June 2007.

"You might be interested to know that NAVSOC is now being operated by contractors. NAVSOC underwent a Commercial Activities Study in 2005 and the government bid (called the Agency Tendered Offer) was underbid by a company called Rome Research Corp. Except for some key "Inherently Governmental" positions, all operations will be performed by contractors."

[162] Paul M. Insch, Captain, U.S. Navy. *NAVSOC Command Brief.* Naval Satellite Operations Center. PowerPoint Brief. June 2006. Slide 41.

[163] Naval Satellite Operations Center. *Modern Satellite Operations, NAVSOC Fact Sheet.* http://www.nbvc.navy.mil/navsoc/docs/FactSheet.pdf. NAVSOC Detachment DELTA is located at Schriever Air Force Base in Colorado Springs, Colorado. The Detachment operates a backup Satellite Operations Center (SOC), which shares the load of daily satellite operations with the Headquarters SOC. Detachment DELTA also provides an on-site liaison with the Air Force Satellite Control Network and other units within the 50th Space Wing when required."

1. **Facilities & Locations**

Composition and location of the NAVSOC organization and its detachments are displayed in Figure 1 (Chapter II). The functional control of each of those individual locations is presented in Table 1 of the same chapter. Each of these installations serve the NAVSOC mission and therefore could continue to perform those same missions should the operation of NAVSOC be transferred over to the 50th Space Wing. In fact, all of the NAVSOC remote detachments are co-located with existing Air Force AFSCN locations. Under this proposed reassignment of responsibilities, the 50th Space Wing would take control of all NAVSOC locations and detachments to incorporate existing infrastructure to support their new mission set.

2. **Personnel**

Table 3 (below) outlines NAVSOC manning. Worldwide, the command employs 146 personnel, of which only 28% are active-duty Navy personnel. As holders of Navy-specific space expertise, re-assignment of these personnel to joint or Air Force activities in support of Navy space needs is an obvious alternative. Detailing some of those forces into the 50th Space Wing will aid in this effort and afford the opportunity for continued representation at the appropriate levels. Re-assignment or elimination of civilian and contractor workforce redundant to existing Air Force satellite operations efforts should be accomplished in line with appropriate Department of Defense business practices.

LOCATION	OFFICERS	ENLISTED	CIVILIANS	On-Site Support	TOTAL
California	8	13	48	43	112
Maine	1	10	3	*5	19
Guam	1	7	0	1	9
Colorado	1	0	3	2	6
TOTAL	11	30	54	51	146

Table 3. NAVSOC Manning Breakdown as of 2006[3]

---

[3] Paul M. Insch, Captain, U.S. Navy. *NAVSOC Command Brief*. Naval Satellite Operations Center. PowerPoint Brief. June 2006. Slide 11.

3. Operations

Daily operations depicted in Figure 8 (below) show the standard daily functions performed by NAVSOC.

"A Day in the Life..."
Satellites / Payloads / Contacts

Constellation	#	Mission – Payloads		Average Contacts Per Day
UFO	8	COMM - 10 UHF/8 EHF/3 GBS	(TT&C)	140
FLTSAT	2	COMM - 2 UHF/2 EHF COMM	(TT&C)	45
POLAR	2	COMM - 2 EHF	(T&C)	1
GFO	1	METOC - Radar Altimetry	(TT&C)	13
NIMS	4	Research – Doppler	(T&C)	8
Totals	17	31		207

— Naval Satellite Operations Center —— Underway With The Fleet, Supporting the Joint Warfighter — 30

Figure 8. A Snap Shot of Daily Operations at NAVSOC[164]

Clearly, when contrasted with the massive volume of Air Force Satellite Control Network daily events (more than 10,000 per day), the small quantity of systems and contact events the NAVSOC manages pose no impediment to the Air Force absorbing these functions. The scope of 14th Air Force efforts in space systems operations as described below is approximately two orders of magnitude greater than Navy efforts:

> The 14th Air Force is comprised of five wings and a Joint Space Air Operations Center (JSpOC), including 155 units at 44 locations worldwide. The 50th Space Wing is located at Schriever Air Force Base, Colo., and operates satellite control centers at Schriever AFB, and

---
[164] Paul M. Insch, Captain, U.S. Navy. *NAVSOC Command Brief*. Naval Satellite Operations Center. PowerPoint Brief. June 2006. Slide 30.

command and control facilities and remote tracking stations around the world. These control centers monitor satellites during launch, early orbit tests, and operate the satellites while they are in orbit and fix satellite anomalies when they occur. Crew members conduct 24-hour operations to monitor the status of and control satellite systems. The Air Force Satellite Control Network (AFSCN) consists of eight subordinate tracking stations located around the world and provides on-orbit tracking, telemetry, commanding and mission data retrieval services to support the NASA, civil, allied, and DoD satellite operations. The satellite systems the wing operates include the NAVSTAR Global Positioning System, the Defense Satellite Communications System, NATO/Skynet, and Milstar. The wing also supports the Defense Support Program, Mid-course Space Experiment, NASA's Advanced Composition Explorer, and the Defense Meteorological Satellite Program, as well as manages the Air Force Satellite Control Network. The wing is made up of approximately 3,200 military, civilians and contract personnel in its workforce.[165]

Incorporating NAVSOC operations into 14th Air Force and 50th Space Wing, responsibilities streamlines the organizational command and control of SATCOM systems, and enables greater simplicity in the overall U.S. space architecture.

4. Benefits

What does the Navy gain from the daily operations at NAVSOC? There is no clear evidence that indicates NAVSOC can produce a superior level of service or higher system reliability than the Air Force. Allocation of the resources provided by NAVSOC spacecraft payloads is not under NAVSOC control, so Naval users derive no capability benefit from NAVSOC operations. NAVSOC itself claims a lower cost-per-satellite operation rate than the 50th Space Wing,[166] and greater efficiencies in common computer interface control of multiple satellite platforms[167] but these arguments fail to take into account the elimination of mult-service administrative overhead, and some of the more

---

[165] Department of the Air Force. *14th Air Force Fact Sheet.* http://www.vandenberg.af.mil/library/factsheets/factsheet.asp?id=4684. 20 June 2007.

[166] Paul M. Insch, Captain, U.S. Navy. *NAVSOC Command Brief.* Naval Satellite Operations Center. PowerPoint Brief. June 2006. Slide 41.

[167] Joel Hicks. Commander, U.S. Navy. Email to the authors: *Re: Questions regarding NAVSOC.* 15 June 2007. NAVSOC operates all of their satellites on a common Integrated Satellite Control System (ISCS), meaning that monitoring and commanding can be performed on a single operating system.

recent Air Force initiatives in fielding consolidated command and control systems.[168] The sole advantage to the presence of a Naval Satellite Operations entity seems to be the institutional prestige inherent in the tradition of Navy space operations.

In contrast, incorporation of NAVSOC missions into the Air Force satellite C^2 architecture eliminates a non-core business from the Navy's slate of missions, centralizes responsibility and authority for the operation of space systems, simplifies funding and administration and eliminates redundancy. Further, proper consideration and construction of multi-service positions within the Air Force's satellite control organizations could open the door to improved representation and fulfillment of service-specific needs with regards to satellite resources and products.

Existing friction among the services with regards to the role of satellite resources service providers and satellite resources consumers is a recognized problem with this organizational construct, and the topic is deserving of more than a hand-waving approach. In-depth study of that issue is, however, beyond the scope of this paper. Considering the existing overwhelming "market share" the Air Force possesses in its role as a supplier of satellite resources to the other military services, continuation of this trend to its logical conclusion poses no great intellectual leap. Addressing the complaints of the satellite user community may require a completely new organizational structure internal to the Air Force, or possibly a new structure external to existing organizations, with a focus and mission dedicated to support to the forward-deployed satellite system user.

C. NAVY OPERATIONAL SPACE SUPPORT

NETWARCOM's Maritime Operations Center is a recently founded and renamed organization, located at NETWARCOM headquarters in Little Creek, Virginia. Established as the NIOSC "fusion center" in 2005, the renamed NNWC MOC:

> …is a brand new, state-of-the-art operations center that will manage worldwide naval operational and technical support across strategic,

---

[168] David Ulrich, Colonel, U.S. Air Force. *MILSATCOM Satellite Communications Overview Brief.* PowerPoint Brief. June 2007. Slide 13.

operational and tactical levels. Ultimately, the NIOSC (sic.) will promote data sharing and foster an environment of collaboration required to plan and respond to current and future threats.[169]

The NNWC MOC Space Cell missions vis-à-vis space operations include:

...functions as a true reachback staff element for deployed Strike Groups and forward Maritime Headquarters. The space planners in the NIOSC (sic.) broker maritime operational and exercise space needs with the Joint Space Operations Center at Vandenberg AFB and assist the theater Space Coordinating Authorities as they develop the space support requests for their AORs. This insures that the desired DoD and National Technical space effects are delivered in support of Fleet activities.[170]

Without consideration of the NetOps and Information Operations missions, the space-coordination function, embodied in a sub-unit of the NNWC MOC called the "Space Cell" is completely superfluous and redundant to the Joint Space Operations Center (JSpOC). Navy forces reachback for space support, planning and effects through the Space Cell introduces a completely unnecessary layer to the space support hierarchy and re-directs information flow through an additional, needless loop. (Refer to Figure 5, page 49).

The NNWC MOC Space Cell is critically dependent upon space-related information provided and brokered by the JSpOC, and serves only as a conduit and middleman to transfer that information to afloat forces. The Space Cell, upon receiving requests for information from maritime users, merely reaches to the JSpOC with the query, and then forwards the JSpOC-sourced information back to the user who made the original request. Further, joint manning requirements designed to support the full spectrum of users – ground forces, afloat units and air forces – have already been implemented at the JSpOC, with attendant attention paid to the need for maritime-specific expertise on the watch-floor.

---

[169] Dean Wence. *Increasing the Fleet's Capabilities with Reach Back.* CHIPS. October-December 2005 Issue. http://www.chips.navy.mil/archives/05_oct_dec/web_pages/maritime_center.htm. June 2007.

[170] James D. McArthur, Admiral, U.S. Navy. *Statement Before the Strategic Forces Subcommittee of the Senate Armed Services Committee on FY 2008 Defense Budget Authorization Request for Space Activities.* 19 April 2007. http://armed-services.senate.gov/statemnt/2007/April/McArthur%2004-19-07.pdf. June 2007.

The logical and proper information structure eliminates the NNWC Space Cell from the loop, with maritime users reaching directly to the JSpOC for space resource assistance. To allay the concerns of the Navy user regarding defense of Navy-specific space requirements, manning adjustments at the JSpOC should be considered, with increased numbers and insertion of appropriate expertise sourced from the Navy Space Cadre. This solution poses a win-win from the perspective of both the Air Force space operations community and the Navy Space Cadre, providing needed personnel for manning, cross-cultural training and experience for the Space Cadre, and multi-service legitimacy for the JSpOC as operational usage increases.

The need for NETWARCOM's internal situational awareness with regards to Navy space efforts could be fielded by the refinement of the space function within the NNWC MOC. A single watch station or terminal dedicated to providing critical space-related information to NETWARCOM decision makers could draw on resources at the JSpOC as needed. In turn, the fostering of a robust Navy presence or Space Cell within the JSpOC will provide greater fluidity in the dissemination of operational Navy space needs. The removal of the NNWC MOC Space Cell from the operational support information path streamlines the efforts of the forward-deployed Naval space user. The effectiveness of Space Cadre members in performing operational space support is enhanced by the ability to reach back to a single point of contact within the joint space world. Further, enhanced Navy presence in the JSpOC provides timely and influential input regarding Navy space needs and requirements within the JSpOC's joint working environment.

Elimination of the NNWC MOC Space Cell and attendant organizational redundancy poses no threat to the distribution of resources and information required by the space-enabled Navy, and indeed, presents a more streamlined and efficient path for space information distribution.

D. **NAVY SATELLITE SYSTEMS ACQUISITION**

Overarching policy direction for the armed forces to participate in space systems acquisition is included in DoDD 5101.2, the DoD Executive Agent for Space directive. This document mandates that:

> 6.3. The Heads of the DoD Components shall:
>
> 6.3.7 Continue to develop, acquire, and fund space research, development and acquisition programs that meet DoD Component requirements and submit such program information to the DoD Executive Agent for Space in accordance with this Directive.[171]

The Department of the Navy Space Policy requires participation in National Security Space organization activities, to include acquisition *when appropriate*.[172] In line with these requirements, the Program Executive Office (PEO) Space Systems was established in May 2004, and charged with the coordination of all Department of the Navy space research, development and acquisition activities.[173] Reporting to PEO Space Systems is the Communications Satellite Program Office, PMW-146, whose mission it is to "acquire space based communications systems for the fleet and joint users."[174]

PEO Space Systems more generally works to coordinate with the Under Secretary of the Air Force and the National Reconnaissance Office to ensure the Navy is purchasing appropriate space systems to support the larger National Security Space goals. PMW-146 is the only directorate reporting directly to PEO Space Systems, and is directly responsible for the acquisition and fielding of communications-specific satellite capabilities.

---

[171] United States. Department of Defense Directive 5101.2, *DoD Executive Agent for Space.* July 2003. Section 6.3. http://www.dtic.mil/whs/directives/corres/html/510102.htm. June 2007.

[172] Department of the Navy. SECNAV Instruction 5400.39C: *Department of Navy Space Policy*. 6 April 2004. Section 4b.(3)(a). http://ftp.fas.org/irp/doddir/navy/secnavinst/5400_39c.pdf. April 2007. Emphasis added.

[173] Department of the Navy. SPAWAR PEO Space Systems Webpage. http://enterprise.spawar.navy.mil/body.cfm?type=c&category=26&subcat=54. June 2007.

[174] Department of the Navy. SPAWAR Website. http://enterprise.spawar.navy.mil/pd14/PMW146/Mission/mission_statement.htm. June 2007.

1. **Background and Specifics**

While PEO Space Systems is relatively new, PMW-146 is a historical outgrowth of Naval Research Laboratory work on the *FLTSATCOM* project in the early 1970s.[175] PMW-146 has executed the acquisition and fielding of all of the modern Department of Defense narrowband (UHF) satellite systems under the Navy's charter as the lead agency for narrowband. PMW-146 is currently focused primarily on the task of fielding the Mobile User Objective System (*MUOS*), the upcoming generation of UHF communications satellites. The effort for design and acquisition of *MUOS* is lauded as a high-quality acquisition program amidst a panoply of spectacular failures in space systems acquisition.[176]

PMW-146 was rolled under the new PEO Space Systems when that organization was stood up in 2004. The establishment of a Program Executive Office for Space was an outgrowth of increasing attention in the Department of the Navy to space issues following the 2001 Space Commission Report and a desire to centralize the functions that support space systems and operations within the Navy. In a sense, it is a similar construct to the Navy Space Systems Division, OP943, which was chartered in 1981, and resulted in the Naval Postgraduate School Space Systems Operations and Engineering degree programs, and Space Subspecialty billet codes.[177] PEO Space, however, has inter-agency coordination requirements for a persistent relationship with the Under Secretary of the Air Force for the purposes of space systems acquisition.[178]

---

[175] Navy Communications Satellite Programs Fact Sheet. Ultra High Frequency Follow-On (UFO) Program. 1 March 1999. http://www.globalsecurity.org/space/library/report/1999/uhf_follow-on_fact_sheet.pdf. June 2007. Gary Federici. *From the Sea to the Stars*. Naval Historical Center. July 2003. Section 3.3.4. http://www.history.navy.mil/books/space/index.htm. May 2007

[176] Taylor Dinerman. *The U.S. Navy: lost in space?* The Space Review. 24 October 2005. http://www.thespacereview.com/article/480/1. June 2007. Taylor Dinerman. *United States Space Force: sooner rather than later* 27 February 2006. .http://www.thespacereview.com/article/565/1. June 2007. Witness the disasters in the TSAT and SBR programs.

[177] Gary Federici. *From the Sea to the Stars*. Naval Historical Center. July 2003. Section 4.1. http://www.history.navy.mil/books/space/index.htm. May 2007

[178] United States. *National Security Space Acquisition Policy. 03-1*. Department of Defense. 27 December 2004.

2. True Acquisition Reform...

Regardless of the relative success of the *MUOS* program and history of narrowband satellite expertise, the Navy no longer has the motives to champion UHF communications that brought it into the narrowband satellite communications arena in the 1970s. When UHF satellite communications were conceived, they were intended to provide afloat users with very narrow bandwidth command and control links via the Information Exchange Subsystem[179] family of satellite links. UHF was chosen as an appropriate frequency range because it permitted installation of reasonably small antennas on the already crowded superstructure of ships. Today, bandwidth requirements shipboard far exceed the ability of UHF to deliver data. Instead, the disadvantaged mobile user, typically assessed as troops on the ground, is the intended beneficiary of the "last-mile" *MUOS* system. In an environment where more than 90% of satellite control and operation efforts are accomplished by the Air Force, and Navy forces' reliance on UHF is superseded by commercial and high-bandwidth systems, might not the Navy relieve itself of this program?

DoD Directive 5101.2 identifies eight major responsibilities for the individual service components to accomplish with regard to National Security Space programs. Of these eight responsibilities, a committee of the Naval Studies Board identifies four (including the responsibility for acquisition programs) as having "...little or no evidence of responsive naval management actions."[180] The Naval Studies board uses this critical evaluation to advocate increased emphasis across the entire spectrum of requirements of the 2001 DoD Directive, yet manpower and resources to accomplish the entirety of that effort are not identified and presumably unavailable, as current Department of Defense priorities are rather more focused on the immediate challenges of the Global War on

---

[179] TADIXS, http://www.globalsecurity.org/intell/systems/tadixs.htm. OTCIXS, http://www.globalsecurity.org/intell/library/reports/2001/compendium/OTCIXS.htm, SSIXS, http://www.globalsecurity.org/wmd/systems/ssixs.htm

[180] National Research Council. Committee on the Navy's Needs in Space for Providing Future Capabilities. *The Navy's Needs in Space for Providing Future Capabilities*. The National Academies Press 2005. p. 68.. http://books.nap.edu/openbook.php?record_id=11200&page=68. June 2007.

Terrorism. Instead, divestiture of this apparently inadequate and redundant acquisition effort by the Navy will permit more appropriate focus of resources on other Department of Defense space requirements.

In the same way that the various services should turn to the Air Force as the service provider for satellite operations and bandwidth, so should the Navy relinquish its development and acquisition of satellite systems to the Air Force. With "historical imperative" as the primary rationale for continuing to field and acquire satellites, the Navy needs to divest itself of this non-core operation.

Programmatic funding and reallocation is a concern under this construct. Planned annual unclassified Navy expenditures on space-related activities each year between FY 2004 and FY 2009 are approximately $1.3 billion. Nearly 90% of these funds support Navy satellite communications, but more specifically, program operation and acquisition of narrowband satellite communications comprises almost 50%.

The Navy's space-related budget is allocated to the following:[181]

- Communications satellites (*UFO, MUOS*), 49.8%
- Satellite communications terminals, 38.7%
- NAVSOC, 5.2%
- Global Positioning System receivers and equipment, 2.8%
- Spectrum management and interference reduction, 1.5%
- Navy TENCAP and the Ground Moving Target Indication Advance Concept Technology Demonstration, 1.1%
- Meteorology and oceanography, 0.9%
- Missile warning, 0.005%

Transfer of the communication satellites line item from Navy PEO Space and PMW-146 control to the Air Force's Space and Missile Center (SMC) will likely represent a complete loss of these funds for the Navy. In an era of ballooning expenditures for support of day-to-day combat operations and tightly controlled budgets

---

[181] National Research Council. Committee on the Navy's Needs in Space for Providing Future Capabilities. *The Navy's Needs in Space for Providing Future Capabilities*. The National Academies Press 2005. p. 23. http://books.nap.edu/openbook.php?record_id=11200&page=23. June 2007.

across the Department of Defense, the panorama of overall DoD outlays must take precedence over service-specific programs and turf battles. In the National Security Space "big-picture" view, transfer of these narrowband satellite communication programs to Air Force control may achieve cost savings in the aggregation of related missions with existing programs at SMC. Redundancies in overhead, from administration to physical infrastructure and facilities are easily identified, and encompass only a thumbnail sketch of savings when compared to potential efficiencies gained through process and production standardization.

While the shift of programmatic and acquisition responsibilities to the Air Force represents a loss of funds to the Navy, recovery of the human resources from PEO Space and PMW-146 presents an excellent opportunity for the strengthening of both the Navy Space Cadre as well as the real historical core competency[182] of the Navy's space efforts – scientific research and technology development.

E. REINVORGATION OF NAVY SPACE S&T AND UTILIZATION OF THE NAVAL RESEARCH LABORATORY

As evidenced by the vast array and number of awards and accomplishments garnered by the Naval Research Laboratory (NRL), the organization has served the Navy well as the preeminent developer of space and science and technology research for the enterprise.[183] From initial high altitude atmospheric research, to the fielding of the *Vanguard* program in response to the launch of *Sputnik* in 1957, the NRL has a legacy of space systems development stretching back more than a half century. Though it yielded up its rocket design expertise to NASA in 1958, continuation of research and development efforts in orbital systems established a superlative reputation for engineering expertise and rigorous space science. A variety of internal re-structuring, divisional re-coding and re-naming have occurred since the late 1950s, however, the

---

[182] Gary Federici. *From the Sea to the Stars*. Naval Historical Center. July 2003. Various. http://www.history.navy.mil/books/space/index.htm. May 2007. Summary verbiage in Chapter 5 emphasizes the U.S. Navy's scientific legacy and "long pole of technical and scientific competence." http://www.history.navy.mil/books/space/index.htm.

[183] Department of the Navy, Naval Research Laboratory Website. http://www.nrl.navy.mil/content.php?P=PATENTS. June 2007.

present form of NRL's space science and technology organization has been in existence since 1986. In October of that year, the Space Systems and Technology division was renamed the Naval Center for Space Technology (NCST), and assigned oversight duties for the Space Systems Development Department, the Spacecraft Engineering Department, and the Space Systems Technology Department.[184]

1. Mission & Focus of Effort

Specifically included in the mission statement for the NRL with regards to space is identification of its position within the Department of the Navy:

- "Serves as the lead Navy activity for space technology and space systems development and support."

…and…

NRL, the Navy's single, integrated Corporate Laboratory, provides the Navy with a broad foundation of in-house expertise from scientific through advanced development activity. Specific leadership responsibilities are assigned in the following areas:...

- Space and space systems technology, development, and support.[185]

A fairly small organization, employing approximately 2500 personnel, the NRL has a narrower focus on research and science than the existing organizations responsible for developing, acquiring and operating space technology. NCST efforts, and related NRL work – in space environments, space science, high-bandwidth communications, and remote sensing – are more accurately aligned with the Navy's traditional "leveraged funding"[186] and "ruthless customer" paradigm than the large-scale programmatics of the existing Program Executive Office system in place.

---

[184] Department of the Navy. Naval Research Laboratory Website, NCST Homepage. *The Origin of NCST*. http://ncst-www.nrl.navy.mil/NCSTOrigin/NCSTOrigin2.html. June 2007.

[185] Department of the Navy. Naval Research Laboratory Website. http://www.nrl.navy.mil/content.php?P=MISSION. June 2007.

[186] Gary Federici. *From the Sea to the Stars*. Naval Historical Center. July 2003. Section 4.14.1. http://www.history.navy.mil/books/space/index.htm. May 2007.

95

The Naval Center for Space Technology is positioned and focused to perform fundamental advanced science and technology for both the Navy and the greater National Security Space community. Without the burden of needing to support Navy-specific acquisition, personnel and efforts could be used to fulfill Navy needs in space[187] at the technology development level rather than the systems deployment level. Use of this extensive intellectual talent pool with relief from the political considerations and Byzantine maneuvering of systems acquisition permits more productive research, with corresponding improvements in systems refinement and development time. Additionally, technology transfer is simplified in this model. With all Navy space technology under development in-house at NCST, and all contracting and acquisition taking place at the Air Force's Space and Missile Center, communication requirements for multiple R&D and contracting organizations are eliminated. Further, protocols between these two expert organizations, working exclusively within their area of competence, might be simplified, and partnering relationships taking advantage of the authoritative nature of each organization could be constructed.

2. Recovery of Capabilities

Intelligence Satellite Development by the Naval Research Laboratory

In a sense, the Naval Research Laboratory (NRL) became a victim of its own success. Beginning in 1960, the nation's investment in space-based systems expanded tremendously. The expansion was far beyond anything that an organization even as large as NRL could cope with. Although NRL developed and launched some 80 satellites in the four decades between 1960 and 2000, the number was only 1 or 2 percent of the total national effort. NRL's expertise in sensor technology and scientific research caused the expertise of its staff to be sought out and funded by a long list of non-Navy organizations (the Air Force, Army, Missile Defense Agency, National Aeronautics and Space Administration, National Oceanic and Atmospheric Administration, National Security Agency, National Reconnaissance Office (NRO), National Science Foundation, predecessors of the National Geospatial-Intelligence Agency, and others). The support that NRL received from all of these non-Navy organizations was sufficient to allow it to build up a large and very competent staff.

---

[187] Department of the Navy. Memorandum for Under Secretary of the Air Force/Executive Agent for Space. *Navy Space Needs*. 13 February 2006.

Through the early 1980s, NRL's largest effort was in support of the development of classified prototype surveillance satellites. These developments were indeed successful, to the degree that the sponsoring agency (NRO) decided to go into serial production of such satellites. Since NRL was a research laboratory and not a manufacturing facility, the production of the next generation of satellites was transferred to an industrial organization. This transfer left many members of the NRL staff without sponsor support and necessitated a rather traumatic drawdown in the number of NRL personnel available to manage the development, acquisition, and launch of full satellite systems. The difficulty was that the Navy (through the Office of Naval Research) only provided funds to cover NRL's basic research activities. In the past three decades, no Navy funds have been provided to NRL to develop and launch new satellite systems. As a consequence, NRL's ability to develop and deploy satellite systems that offer the Navy new warfighting capabilities has diminished by a significant amount.[188]

Returning the Navy to active participation, funding and use of its own premier space systems research and development organization is a crucial step in centralizing and simplifying the complex mish-mash of space systems requirements articulation, capabilities experimentation and systems design and development. Through a renaissance in S&T, and recognition of that function as a core competency of the Navy's space efforts, representation of the Navy's needs in space can be more clearly articulated to organizations acting as service providers.

3. Human Capital Re-Use

In addition to the Navy-provided funding required to re-invigorate the NRL and NCST, use of the talent pool and expertise currently scattered throughout Program Offices within the NRO and the Navy is imperative.[189] NETWARCOM, in its 2007 Strategic Plan, establishes a goal to:

- *Ensure Navy fully leverages and influences Space capabilities.*

With the following major supporting strategies:

---

[188] National Research Council. Committee on the Navy's Needs in Space for Providing Future Capabilities. *The Navy's Needs in Space for Providing Future Capabilities.* The National Academies Press 2005. Appendix A. p.157. http://books.nap.edu/openbook.php?record_id=11200&page=157. June 2007.

[189] Taylor Dinerman. *The U.S. Navy: lost in space?* The Space Review. 24 October 2005. http://www.thespacereview.com/article/480/1. June 2007.

- Improve human capital: Cultivate Navy Sapce Cadre expertise for assignment in Navy, as well as Joint space and national Security Space (NSS) billets.

- Ingrain cultural change: Harvest space-related best practices from Naval Space Campaign lessons learned and institutionalize them through doctrine and policy.[190]

Use of Navy Space Cadre officers, reassigned PEO Space and PMW-146 personnel, and pure science and technology researchers within the umbrella of the Naval Research Laboratory provides an opportunity for cross-cultural learning, improved communication between system developers and warfighters, clearer understanding of system capabilities and limitations, and ultimately, more complete, accurate and lucid requirements definition to the Air Force in an acquisition and service provider role.

Revitalization of the role of the NRL and NCST as the "center of excellence" for Navy Space provides not only an organizational hub for the ad-hocracy that describes the larger Navy Space organization, but also supports Department of Defense requirements to maintain space skills in an expert cadre.[191] Formalization of the Navy's focus for space within the realm of science and technology, with corollary requirements in experimentation and technology transfer, demands levels of expertise not only in the academic environment, but also within the uniformed members of the Space Cadre. Rotation of military, and even civilian scientists, from within the developmental center of the NCST to a variety of jobs in fields such as operational requirements definition and systems acquisition provides for a broad-spectrum distribution of knowledge, skills and critical abilities. Additionally, unification of personnel who provide expertise in requirements generation with technical experts provides a method to allay fears of lack of Navy involvement during the requirements definition phase of the acquisition process. Through proper positioning of these key, cross-trained personnel within joint acquisition

---

[190] Department of the Navy. *Naval Network Warfare Command Strategic Plan. Executive Summary, Version 2.0.* Naval Network Warfare Command. 23 March 2007. p.12. Cited strategies comprise only two of eight identified initiatives.

[191] United States. Department of Defense Directive 5101.2, *DoD Executive Agent for Space.* July 2003. Section 6.3.5. http://www.dtic.mil/whs/directives/corres/html/510102.htm. June 2007.

and program offices, the Navy Space Cadre can be used to defend Navy interests in large national and DoD satellite programs throughout their entire lifecycle.

F. SELLING THE FARM…AND BUYING A NEW ONE.

Navy efforts in the broad spectrum of space endeavors for much of the last two decades have been decentralized, fragmented and characterized by a lack of rudder authority. Alignment of operational Navy space efforts under NETWARCOM at its inception in 2002 exacerbated the drift in Navy space functions as that organization struggled with its initial sense of mission and the demands of a newly "network-centric" operating concept. Large-scale Navy policy efforts from 2002 on have been largely predicated on the concept of Sea Power 21. This four-part strategy relies both in part and in its entirety on products, services and capabilities provided by space systems. Within the space products and capabilities required by Sea Power 21 are a variety of Navy-unique requirements, without which the construct becomes unworkable. Analysis of critical dependencies on space infrastructure indicate that, without clear and unambiguous requirements definition on the part of the Navy for future space systems, participation in future conflicts will be restricted by unmet needs.[192] Under the existing hash of internal and external acquisition procedures and agencies, satellite operations and resource providers, and Navy specific space requirements generation processes,[193] the Navy's needs for space-provided resources will clearly not be met.

It is time for the Navy to transfer its programmatic and acquisition efforts to another agency, and invest exclusively in a two pronged approach consisting of science and technology R&D and the promotion of a robust, effective Navy Space Cadre. The alternative is for the concentration of effort in Navy space to remain unfocused, irrelevant, and mired in historical raison d'être.

---

[192] National Research Council. Committee on the Navy's Needs in Space for Providing Future Capabilities. *The Navy's Needs in Space for Providing Future Capabilities.* The National Academies Press 2005. Various. Executive Summary, Chapter 3, Chapter 4. http://books.nap.edu/openbook.php?record_id=11200&page=157. June 2007.

[193] For an overview of the Navy's method of operational input for space related requirements, see *The Navy's Needs in Space for Providing Future Capabilities*, p. 70.

THIS PAGE INTENTIONALLY LEFT BLANK

VI. FINAL CONCLUSIONS AND RECOMMENDATIONS

A. THESIS SUMMARY

Navy efforts in the space arena have a storied history and comprise a valued contribution to national security space efforts. Achievements of the past permit the prestige of the present, but it is time to look to the future from the perspective of appropriate resource use, not nostalgia. In line with the current Department of Defense force transformation and restructuring, U.S. Navy space efforts are in a state of flux. Prompted by policy requirements and a sort of institutional peer-pressure, the Navy's space community has attempted to maintain a certain status within the DoD, ease pressures coming from Capital Hill regarding the need for a Space Cadre, and perpetuate an institutional legacy of space excellence. In this venture, however, the selected approach and accepted organizational goals lie at cross purposes with sober business considerations and functionality. The time has come for the Navy to relinquish its redundant operational control of communication satellites and re-focus on science and technology research. Secondly, current efforts by NETWARCOM and senior Navy leadership to establish a solid Navy Space Cadre fall short when compared to other services' efforts. The future success of Navy space is dependent on the growth and empowerment of a vigorous Navy Space Cadre. Finally, to ensure the maximum effectiveness of future Navy space efforts, the Navy must redefine its role in the acquisition process by eliminating the PEO Space Systems office, to include PMW-146, and reinvest in the NRL, ensuring continuation of necessary S&T research and advancements. These proposed restructuring efforts can pave the way to the realization of the full potential of the Navy space enterprise.

In an effort to aid in the decision-making process required to contemplate such a proposal, exposure to the definitions, concepts, instructions and policies associated with the Naval Space Campaign is required. Current Department of Defense and Department of the Navy policy statements are a constructive step in promoting the necessary and critical nature of space operations and have produced positive, but limited results. Unfortunately, the high-level statements lack sufficient clarity in some areas, and that ambiguity has resulted in a lack of accomplishment in some details. The establishment of NETWARCOM as the Navy Space Type Commander, formalization of the Navy Space Cadre, composition of the Naval Space Campaign, and the trial run of the first ever CSG Staff Space Officer comprise highlights of Navy space efforts in the face of vague doctrine and apparent senior-level disinterest. Additional clarity in the Navy space doctrinal library regarding an implementation strategy and consolidated Navy space architecture is needed, as well as leadership involvement and guidance in the joint space environment.

Literature regarding DoD space cadre activity has been critical of the U.S. Navy's efforts in establishing and implementing an effective strategy for their space cadre program. As a response to the 2001 Space Commission report, the Secretary of the Navy mandated the establishment of a 'cross-community' Navy Space Cadre to meet requirements stated in that document and subsequent DoD Directive 5101.2. From the beginning, the Navy Space Cadre has been considered a subspecialty occupation, secondary to the individual's primary profession. Currently there are approximately 800 active duty officers, 120 reserve officers and 300 civilian personnel that make up the cadre. Though the Navy Space Cadre Advisors have recently made strides to improve the Navy's utilization of the expertise contained within the membership of its cadre, the Navy still lags other services' space efforts. Disregard of this state of affairs at senior levels seems to be endemic, perhaps overshadowed by other pressing concerns of institutional mission, asymmetric warfare and budget struggles. Proposals for cost-savings and more efficient human capital use would therefore seem to be timely and appropriate. Proper utilization of the Navy Space Cadre is a continuous struggle. The detailing processes, creation of billets and training/education have plagued cadre leadership, and pose a roadblock to the task of building and maintaining a robust space cadre.

In the traditional, blue-water mission area, the Navy Space Cadre is just beginning to receive operational employment. Recent undertakings by the first CSG Staff Space Officer have provided the cadre with a senior, operational commander convinced of the importance of space effects for the seagoing military force. Leverage of this operational advocacy provides the necessary muscle to influence future deliberations regarding the need for Navy Space Cadre use, improvements and growth. The Navy Space Cadre's ongoing struggle for validation and respect will continue until senior Navy leadership recognizes space as an indispensable 'force multiplier' and allocates resources commensurate with that status.

The Navy should establish new, more efficient and cost effective methods to achieve its requirements for space effects. The current construct for operation and control of space-borne assets no longer provides tangible benefits to the Navy, and should the Navy transfer possession of these satellites to the Air Force, it would streamline the organizational command and control of SATCOM systems and enable greater simplicity in the overall U.S. space architecture. Additionally, disestablishment of PEO Space Systems and PMW-146 and subsequent reinvestment in science and technology efforts more clearly focus and bound the scope of Navy space efforts. To ensure the Navy's needs and requirements are represented and fielded in this new structure, the Navy must carefully position Navy Space Cadre personnel in key positions to influence and direct Navy space efforts throughout the DoD and civilian space environment.

B.   FURTHER EXPLORATION

The United States has become increasingly reliant on space. Space is a critical center of gravity for the military, as well as a vital link in the modern networked civilian world. Planning and execution of operations, at the strategic, operational and tactical levels are dependent upon space.

> Space power provides military leaders, operators, and planners with enormous force-enhancement effects that multiply joint combat effectiveness in prosecuting theater campaigns. Space systems significantly improve friendly forces' ability to strike at the enemy's heart or COGs, paralyzing an adversary to allow land, sea, and air forces to achieve rapid dominance of the battlespace.[194]

---

[194] Mark E. Harter, Lieutenant Colonel, U.S. Air Force. "10 Propositions Regarding Space Power, The Dawn of a Space Force." Air and Space Journal-Summer 2006. 1 June 2006. http://www.airpower.maxwell.af.mil/airchronicles/apj/apj06/sum06/harter.html. 27 June 2007.

Much work remains to be done with regard to the DoD's future efforts concerning space utilization and exploitation for warfighting. As a medium, the unlimited potential of space has captured the imagination of generations of Americans. Novelists, scientists, filmmakers, and military theorists have all endeavored to address the latent promise of the 'ultimate high ground'. Stupendous effort and study to develop implementable military theories for space use remains, and this thesis only scratches the surface of that narrow, ongoing debate. In the broadest military context, analysis is required to aide in the determination of the direction of future DoD space activities, and as a subset of that work, the Navy's future course in space must be established. This section contains recommended future research in line with that subject.

1. Navy Space Officer (NSO)

Establishment of a separate career path and designation for Navy space-qualified officers is a topic that deserves rigorous analysis. To date, all formal efforts in Navy space personnel management have revolved around the central concept of the 'cross-designator' community. Specific analysis of the strengths and weaknesses of this concept have been touched upon in this thesis, but the full scope and potential impact of founding a separate career path for Navy Space Officers remains unexplored. Arguments for such an approach to future Navy space manning can be categorized in terms of return-on-investment,[195] low opportunity cost,[196] and improved representation within senior leadership forums. Counter-arguments can be framed as cost-benefit relations, overlap with existing community missions,[197] and potential loss of space expertise within line officer communities.

---

[195] Training and education for existing personnel filling space-qualified billets should be considered a sunk cost.

[196] *exempli gratia*: Re-designation of "homeless" officers from disestablished communities like F-14 or S-3 squadrons.

[197] Information Warfare, Intelligence and Information Professional communities already share large numbers of Space-qualified officers with overlapping mission and assignments.

The opportunity for continued research and consideration of a new Navy space designator is available for those that wish to ensure the Navy continues in its efforts to maximize the use of space in support of the fleet.

2. United States Space Force

Though discussion regarding creation of a U.S. Space Force dates back to early debates on the missions of the U.S. Air Force,[198] recent internal Air Force discussion in Air University, National Space Studies Center,[199] and Air Force periodicals has raised the intensity and volume of this dialogue.

> The strength of space contributions in strategic military, commercial, and economic operations is undeniable. Space power is not just a continuation of airpower; space is a unique, distinct, war-fighting medium. Continuing to restrain US space power from developing its own identity, culture, theory, and doctrine is to confine a powerful dimension of war fighting available only through the fourth medium of space. Undisputed combat space power is drawing near, and the United States may be on the brink of unleashing decisive military space operations, ushering in the era of a separate space force. The reality is that, as in the evolution of airpower, the true potential of a nation's military space power will come to fruition only when a separate space force is created, complete with its own space-competent leadership, organization, doctrine, theory, policy, and resources.[200]

A Navy perspective on the subject and potential structure of a U.S. Space Force would be of value to this ongoing debate.

> With its own budget, the space service will be able to concentrate on making sure that all the other services have access to the best space-based

---

[198] Time Magazine. *Aerospace Force?* 17 March 1961. http://www.time.com/time/magazine/article/0,9171,894428,00.html. June 2007.

[199] See the National Space Studies Center website for a consolidated listing of U.S. Space Force and U.S. Air Force discussion: http://space.au.af.mil/cadre.htm.

[200] Mark E. Harter, Lieutenant Colonel, U.S. Air Force. "10 Propositions Regarding Space Power, The Dawn of a Space Force." Air and Space Journal-Summer 2006. 1 June 2006. http://www.airpower.maxwell.af.mil/airchronicles/apj/apj06/sum06/harter.html. 27 June 2007.

support possible. The Army, Navy, Marines, Coast Guard, and others who use America's military space assets will not have to worry about institutional favoritism...[201]

Examination of potential benefits for the United States Navy in regards to the argument for a new Space Force provide an excellent opportunity for future research and should be considered for inclusion in the Space Systems Operations curricula at the Naval Postgraduate School.

C. CONCLUSION

Leadership in modern military space efforts is less about an organization's ability to field equipment and orbital systems, and more about effective and rapid policy implementation, institutional focus and clear, concise requirements definition. In recent years, the Navy has fallen short in these undertakings. Senior Navy leadership seems to perceive space-related missions as an on-demand service, without a grasp of the complexities inherent in the operation of the required architectures. Policy and doctrine, though enunciated at the appropriate levels, lacks clarity and specifics and provides insufficient guidance for the naval planner of space systems. Knowledge and hard-earned experience in naval space operations are rare within the Naval officer corps, and individuals possessed of these qualities are sought after for reasons other than their space know-how.

Efforts like the Naval Space Campaign and Navy Space Cadre Human Capital Strategy are steps in the right direction to correct the deficiencies of current Navy space endeavors. These successes, however, need to be extended through careful refinement of the Navy's overall mission with regard to space. Policy revision, human capital and budgetary allocation and outsourcing of non-core tasks must be considered to enable organizational success as measured by effective, timely and responsive use of space and space effects. The future of the United States Navy's space programs are yet unwritten,

---

[201] Taylor Dinerman. "United States Space Force: Sooner than Later." The Space Review. 27 February 2006. http://www.thespacereview.com/article/565/1. 27 June 2007.

but with a strong investment in its space cadre and redirected efforts supporting fundamental science and technology, that future promises to be as bright as the historical achievements of past.

THIS PAGE INTENTIONALLY LEFT BLANK

APPENDIX: SIGNIFICANT DEFINITIONS

This appendix provides further detail regarding the definitions offered in Chapter II. Some of the definitions have been edited to allow for the most prevalent portions to be viewed. Unedited versions of the definitions can be found in the documents themselves located in the List of References section of this thesis.

A. ORGANIZATIONS

1. January 11, 2001 U.S. Commission to Assess National Security Space Management and Organizations (2001 Space Commission)

The Commission was established pursuant to a provision inserted in the FY2000 National Defense Authorization Act. The Commission met from May-December 2000 and issued its report on January 11, 2001. Members were:

- Donald Rumsfeld (until resigning on being nominated SecDef in December)
- Former Senator Malcolm Wallop (R-WY)
- Duane Andrews, former Asst. SecDef for C4I
- Robert Davis, former Deputy Undersecretary of Defense for Space
- William Graham, former Director of the White House Office of Science and Tech Policy
- General Howell Estes, USAF (Ret.), former commander, U.S. Space Command
- General Ronald Fogleman, USAF (Ret.), former Air Force Chief of Staff
- General Charles Horner, USAF (Ret.) former commander, U.S. Space Command
- Admiral David Jeremiah, USN (Ret.) former Vice Chairman, JCS
- General Tom Moorman, USAF (Ret.), former Air Force Vice Chief of Staff
- General Glenn Otis, USA (Ret.), former CINC, U.S. Army Europe and 7th Army
- LtGeneral Jay Garner, USA (Ret.), former Army Assistant Vice Chief of Staff

109

- Douglas Necessary, former House Armed Services Committee staff member[202]

The recommendations from the commission were as follows:

1. The President should consider establishing space as a national security priority.
2. The President should consider the appointment of a Presidential Space Advisory Board to provide independent advice on developing and employing new space capabilities.
3. The President should direct that a Senior Interagency Group for Space be established and staffed within the National Security Council structure.
4. The Secretary of Defense and the Director of Central Intelligence should meet regularly to address national security space policy, objectives and issues.
5. An Under Secretary of Defense for Space, Intelligence and Information should be established.
6. Assign responsibility for the command of Air Force Space Command to a four-star officer other than CINCSPACE/CINCNORAD [Command-in-Chief U.S. Space Command/Commander-in-Chief North American Aerospace Defense Command. End the practice of assigning only Air Force flight-rated officers to the position of CINCSPACE and CINCNORAD.
7. Assign Air Force Space Command responsibility for providing the resources to execute space research, development, acquisition and operations....Assign the Air Force responsibility to organize, train and equip for prompt and sustained offensive and defensive air and space operations...and designate the Air Force as Executive Agent for Space within the Department of Defense.
8. Assign the Under Secretary of the Air Force as the Director of the National Reconnaissance Office and designate the Under Secretary as the Air Force Acquisition Executive for Space.
9. Direct the Defense Advanced Research Projects Agency and the Services' laboratories to undertake development and demonstration of innovative space technologies and systems for dedicated military missions.
10. Establish a Major Force Program for Space (i.e., a separate budget category).

2. Naval Network Warfare Command

NETWARCOM is the functional component for space to USSTRATCOM and the Navy Space Type Commander. In close coordination with FLTFORCOM, Second Fleet, and carrier and expeditionary strike group commanders, NETWARCOM works to improve fleet combat effectiveness with smarter, more aggressive use of space effects and better

---

[202] Center for Defense Information, *Excerpts from the Report of the Commission to Assess United States National Security Space Management and Organization*. 12 January 2001. http://www.cdi.org/program/issue/document.cfm?DocumentID=1335&IssueID=70&StartRow=1&ListRows=10&appendURL=&Orderby=DateLastUpdated&ProgramID=68&issueID=70. June 2007.

understanding of how space effects support maritime operations. FLTFORCOM designated NETWARCOM as the Naval Space Campaign lead as directed in CNO Guidance 2005. NETWARCOM is also the functional authority for the Navy space cadre, ensuring operational space expertise is increased through the Fleet readiness Training Program and deployments. Naval Satellite Operations Center (NAVSOC) is a subordinate command that operates satellite constellations to provide military UHF narrow-band communications (Fleet Satellite), military UHF narrow-band, EHF and Global Broadcast System communications (UFO Follow-on) and support Ionospheric research. NAVSOC also operates the Geodetic/Geophysical Satellite (GEOSAT) Follow-on radar altimeter satellite that provides ocean surface height information to naval meteorological centers, and polar-orbiting host satellites that provide additional EHF communications to military users.[203]

3. Network, Information Operations, and Space Center Space Cell

The NIOSC Space Cell provides the following effects to both the Commander NETWARCOM and the fleet:

- Space Cell NNWC Internal Support
- Provides Commander, NNWC SSA/Synchronizes with NIOSC IO/NETOPS cells for synergistic effects
- NIOSC Space Cell Relationship to JSpOC:
    - *Coordination, synchronization, advocacy for maritime support requirements as community of interest members*
    - Broker space effects requirements for maritime users
    - Define/refine maritime support requirements and convey impacts to maritime users
- NIOSC Space Cell source for technical data to provide to fleet units
- NIOSC Space Cell's source of SSA (includes threat info and status of blue space forces)
- NIOSC Space Cell Support to MHQ/MOC (Operational level):
    - Reachback
    - Staff planning augmentation (data retrieval, info analysis, COA development)
    - Theater level synchronization of maritime space requirements
- NIOSC Space Cell Support to CSG/ESG (Tactical level):
    - Reachback
    - Staff planning augmentation (data retrieval, info analysis, COA development)
    - Provide tailored support products (SSA, etc.)

---

[203] Department of the Navy. Naval Network Warfare Command Website. http://www.netwarcom.navy.mil/. May 2007.

111

- o Maritime domain focus
- o Low bandwidth compatible
- o Daily Navy Space Brief: Emphasized SSA, focus on any adverse impact to maritime forces
- Space Launch Coordination: Coordination to deconflict ATLAS V launch from Cape Canaveral. Drove scheme of maneuver in JAXOA.
- CENTCOM Joint Space C2 Coordination Efforts:
  - o Initiated coordination between the Joint DS4, JSpOC, NAVCENT Space Ops POC (N39), and CSG-8 to shape and influence the JSTO ISO maritime forces.
- Strike Support: Worked with JSpOC and CSG-8 Space Ops to provide both TACAIR and TLAM required GPS PDOP strike planning packages and coordination for GETS.
- Adversary Space: Research the space capabilities and related tactics of potential adversaries. Described how they could degrade our maritime forces by targeting centers of gravity supported by space capabilities.
- Connectivity/Manning: CSG-8 helped to define Space Cell comm/manning requirements based upon our support requirements.
- Coalition Space CONOPS: Researched possibility of conducting Space Ops at REL CNFC within CENTCOM based on CSG8 requirement.
- Fleet Space Playbook: aka Naval Space Campaign CONOPS, ready for CSG-8 OPTEST deployed.[204]

---

[204] Julie Niedermaier, Commander, U.S. Navy. *Navy Space Cadre Update (SSFA Space Indoctrination)*. PowerPoint Brief. Slide 19. March 2007.

4. **Naval Satellite Operations Center (NAVSOC)**

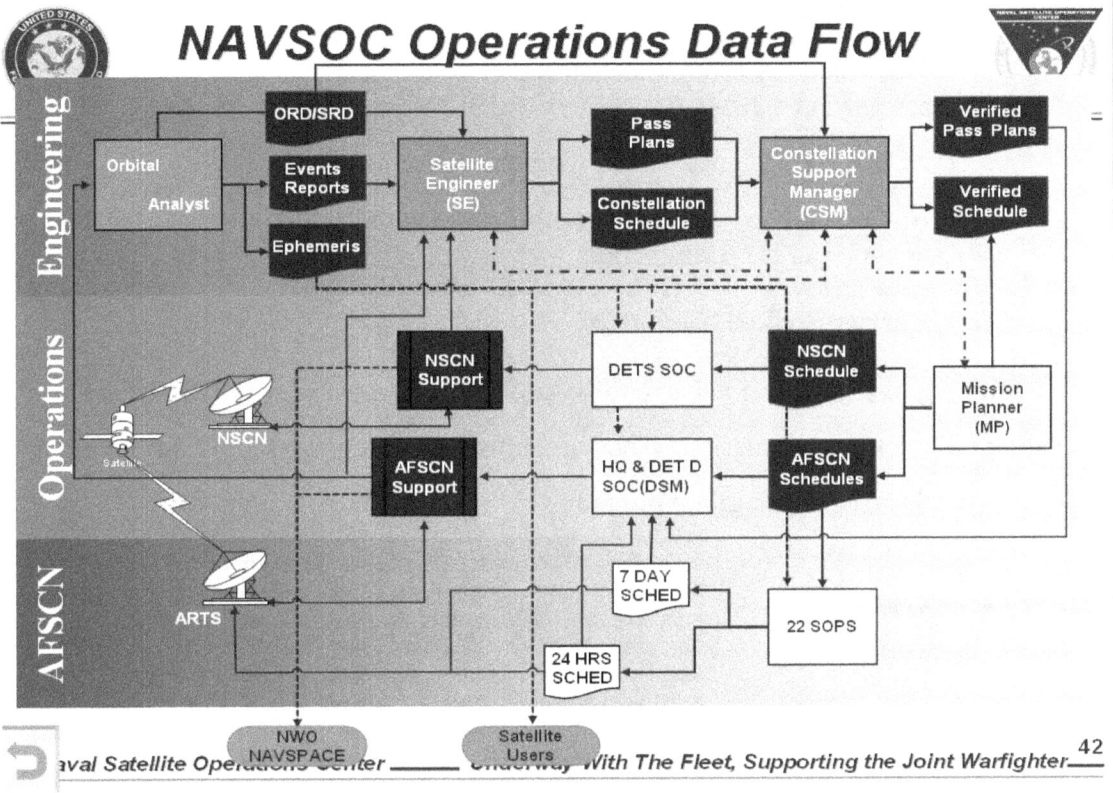

Figure 9. Naval Satellite Operations Center Operations Data Flow Diagram[205]

5. **Maritime Headquarters with Maritime Operations Center (MHQ-MOC)**

The design of the MHQ with MOC fulfills both service management and operational roles with full continuity across the range of military operations. MHQ with MOC allows the maritime commander to perform normal theater-wide operations across the region when no specific Joint Operations Area (JOA) has been established. The MHQ with MOC construct enables operational-level commands to fully support command relationships that could be chosen by a JFC:[206]

- NCC CDR as Service Component Commander with operational control (OPCON)

---

[205] Paul M. Insch, Captain, U.S. Navy. *NAVSOC Command Brief.* Naval Satellite Operations Center. PowerPoint Brief. June 2006. Slide 42.

[206] Department of the Navy. *Maritime Headquarters with Maritime Operations Center Concept of Operations (CONOPS), Final DRAFT Version.* 15 May 2006. p. ii.

- Numbered Fleet commanders and principal headquarters commanders as Service Component Commander with OPCON
- NCC CDR assigned as JFMCC
- Numbered Fleet commanders and principal headquarters commanders assigned as a JFMCC
- NCC CDR assigned as JTF Commander
- Numbered Fleet commanders and principal headquarters commanders assigned as JTF Commander

6. **Carrier Strike Group (CSG)**

Strike groups are formed and disestablished on an as-needed basis, and vary depending on timeline and mission. They are, however, all comprised of similar types of ships. A typical carrier strike group might have:

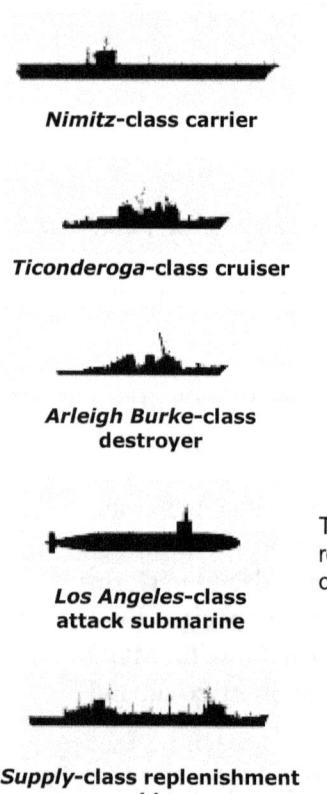

- **a carrier** – The carrier provides a wide range of options to the U.S. government from simply showing the flag to attacks on airborne, afloat and ashore targets. Because carriers operate in international waters, its aircraft do not need to secure landing rights on foreign soil. These ships also engage in sustained operations in support of other forces.
- **a guided missile cruiser** – multi-mission surface combatant. Equipped with *Tomahawks* for long-range strike capability.
- **two guided missile destroyers** – multi-mission surface combatants, used primarily for anti-air warfare (AAW)
- **an attack submarine** – in a direct support role seeking out and destroying hostile surface ships and submarines
- **a combined ammunition, oiler, and supply ship** – provides logistic support enabling the Navy's forward presence; on station, ready to respond

The Carrier Strike Group (CSG) could be employed in a variety of roles, all of which would involve the gaining and maintenance of sea control:

- Protection of economic and/or military shipping.
- Protection of a Marine amphibious force while enroute to, and upon arrival in, an amphibious objective area.
- Establishing a naval presence in support of national interests.

Figure 10. Standard CSG Profile[207]

---

[207] Department of the Navy. *The Carrier Strike Group*. http://www.navy.mil/navydata/ships/carriers/powerhouse/cvbg.asp. June 2007.

7. Joint Space Operations Center (JSpOC)

The primary functions of the JSpOC are:

- Develop a global space operations strategy to meet CDRUSSTRATCOM objectives and guidance.
- Assist development of theater space operations strategy to meet geographic unified commander objectives and guidance through robust interaction with theater AOCs.
- Produce and disseminate the Joint Space Tasking Order (JSTO).
- Task and execute day-to-day space operations for assigned and attached space forces.
- Receive, assemble, analyze, filter and disseminate space-related all-source intelligence and weather information to support air and space operations planning, execution and assessment.
- Conduct operational-level assessments to determine mission and overall space operations effectiveness as required by CDRUSSTRATCOM and other geographic unified combatant commanders to support global and theater combat assessments.[208]

8. Government Accountability Office (GAO)

GAO's primary products are reports, often called "blue books," and testimony before Congress. GAO also issues correspondence (letters), which are narrower in scope, of more limited interest, and do not contain recommendations. With virtually the entire federal government subject to its review, the agency issues a steady stream of products, usually over 900 separate products a year. The agency operates under strict professional standards of review. All numbers and statements of fact presented in GAO work are thoroughly checked and referenced.

Most reports are done at the request of members of Congress--often committee chairpersons and ranking minority members. The agency also responds, whenever possible, to requests from individual members. For example, a senator might ask GAO to examine fraud in the Food Stamp Program. Or a House committee might request a study of a weapon system that is over budget and behind schedule. Other program reviews are required by law or are self-initiated under the agency's own authority.[209]

---

[208] Department of the Air Force. "Air Force Operational Tactics, Techniques, and Procedures 2-3.4, Joint Space Operations Center (Draft)." 20 January 2006.

[209] Government Accountability Office Website. http://www.gao.gov/about/aboutrpt.html. June 2007.

9. **Space and Naval Warfare Systems Command (SPAWAR)**

SPAWARSYSCOM is the Navy's premier Command, Control, Communications, and Computers, Intelligence, Surveillance and Reconnaissance (C4ISR) command for acquisition and life-cycle management of communications and warfare systems. SPAWAR is a dynamic organization, providing world-class information solution to the Warfighters.[210]

10. **Program Executive Office (PEO) Space Systems**

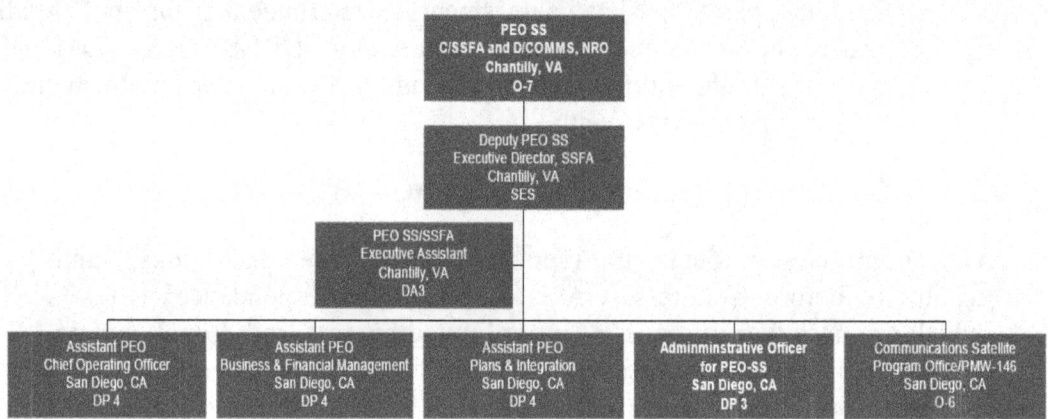

Figure 11. Program Executive Office Space Systems Organizational Chart[211]

---

[210] Department of the Navy. Space and Naval Warfare Systems Command Website. http://www.spawar.navy.mil. May 2007.

[211] Department of the Navy. *PEO Space Systems Missions Statement*. Space and Naval Warfare Systems Command. http://enterprise.spawar.navy.mil/body.cfm?type=c&category=26&subcat=54. May 2007.

11. **Navy Communications Satellite Program Office (PMW-146)**

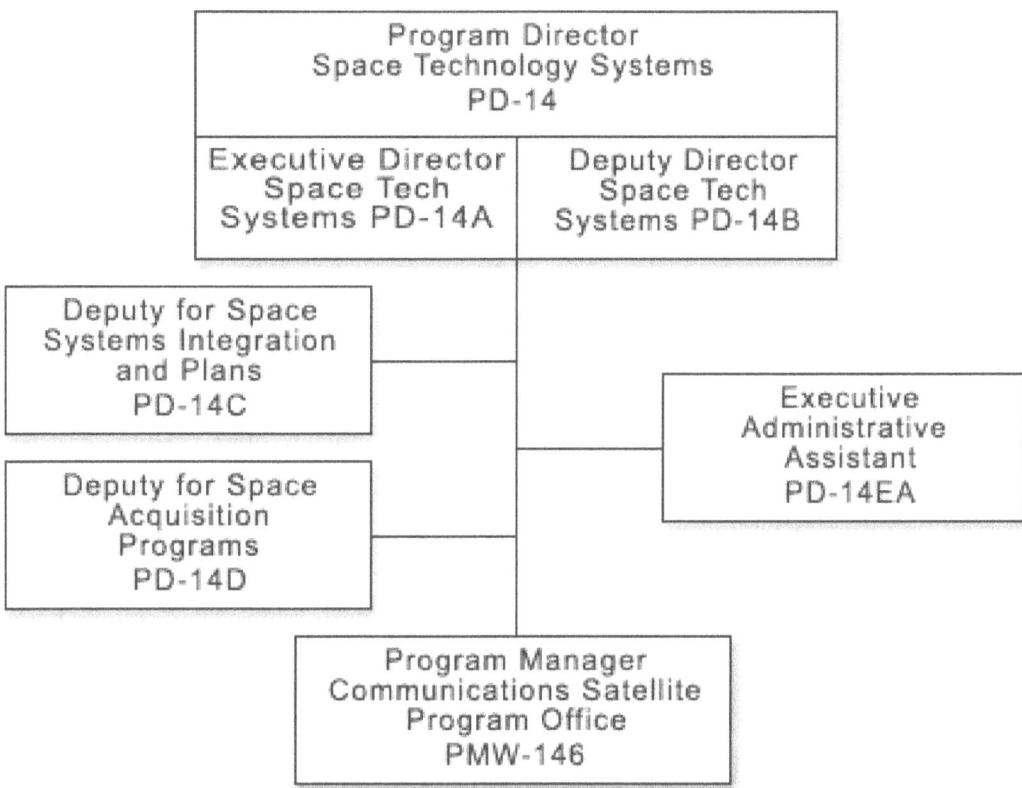

Figure 12. PMW-146 Communications Satellite Programs Office Organizational Chart[212]

12. **National Reconnaissance Office (NRO)**

As part of the 16-member Intelligence Community, the NRO plays a primary role in achieving information superiority for the U. S. Government and Armed Forces.

A DoD agency, the NRO is staffed by DoD and CIA personnel. It is funded through the National Reconnaissance Program, part of the National Foreign Intelligence Program. Vision and Mission: The NRO is guided by

---

[212] Department of the Navy. *PMW-146 Organizational Chart*. Space and Naval Warfare Systems Command. http://enterprise.spawar.navy.mil/pd14/PMW146/index.htm. June 2007.

its vision of being Freedom's Sentinel in Space: One Team, Revolutionizing Global Reconnaissance. Our Mission: The NRO develops and operates unique and innovative overhead reconnaissance systems and conducts intelligence related activities essential for U.S. National Security.[213]

13. Naval Research Laboratories (NRL)

In 1992, the Secretary of the Navy consolidated existing Navy Research, Development, Test and Evaluation Engineering facilities and Fleet Support facilities to form a corporate community. This community consists of a single corporate research laboratory (NRL) aligned with the Office of Naval Research (ONR) and four warfare-oriented centers aligned by mission with the Systems Commands. The four centers are the Naval Air Warfare Center, the Naval Command Control and Ocean Surveillance Center, the Naval Surface Warfare Center, and the Naval Undersea Warfare Center.

As part of the consolidation, the Naval Oceanographic and Atmospheric Research Laboratory, with locations in Stennis Space Center, Mississippi, and Monterey, California, merged with NRL to become what is today, the Navy's corporate laboratory.

Mission: NRL operates as the Navy's full-spectrum corporate laboratory, conducting a broadly based multidisciplinary program of scientific research and advanced technological development directed toward maritime applications of new and improved materials, techniques, equipment, systems and ocean, atmospheric, and space sciences and related technologies. In fulfillment of this mission, NRL:

- Initiates and conducts broad scientific research of a basic and long-range nature in scientific areas of interest to the Navy.
- Conducts exploratory and advanced technological development deriving from or appropriate to the scientific program areas.
- Within areas of technological expertise, develops prototype systems applicable to specific projects.
- Assumes responsibility as the Navy's principal R&D activity in areas of unique professional competence upon designation from appropriate Navy or DOD authority.
- Performs scientific research and development for other Navy activities and, where specifically qualified, for other agencies of the Department of Defense and, in defense-related efforts, for other Government agencies.

---

[213] United States. National Reconnaissance Office Website. http://www.nro.gov/index.html. May 2007.

- Serves as the lead Navy activity for space technology and space systems development and support.
- Serves as the lead Navy activity for mapping, charting, and geodesy (MC&G) research and development for the National Geospatial-Intelligence Agency (NGA).[214]

14.   Navy Center for Space Technology (NCST)

The Space Systems Development Department (SSDD) is the space and ground support systems research and development organization of the Naval Center for Space Technology (NCST). Located at the U.S. Naval Research Laboratory in Washington DC, the primary objective of the SSDD is to develop space systems to respond to Navy, Department of Defense, and national mission requirements with improved performance, capacity, reliability, efficiency, and/or life cycle cost. Together with the Spacecraft Engineering Department (SED), the SSDD derives system requirements from a mission, develops architectures in response to these requirements, and designs and develops systems, subsystems, equipment, and implementation technologies to achieve an optimized, integrated operational space and ground system.[215]

Spacecraft Engineering Department (SED): Under the aegis of the Naval Center for Space Technology (NCST), SED serves as the focal point for the Navy's in-house spacecraft bus capability. Research and development activities range from concept and feasibility studies through initial on-orbit space systems operation. Design, assembly, and test activities are performed in conjunction with NCST's Space Systems Development Department (SSDD). The SED provides analysis, design, and hardware expertise in structures and mechanisms, attitude determination and control systems, propulsion and reaction control systems, thermal control systems, satellite integration and test, launch vehicle integration, and satellite-to-boost-stage integration. The SED functions as the Program Manager for Navy Space Programs. In this role, systems engineering and technical directions are provided while maintaining an active in-house satellite development capability. The SED performs as a prototype laboratory in this role and ensures that designs are transferable to industry for follow-on satellite builds.[216]

---

[214] Department of the Navy. *NRL Missions Statement*. Naval Research Laboratory. http://www.nrl.navy.mil/content.php?P=MISSION. June 2007.

[215] Department of the Navy. *Space Systems Development Department*. Naval Center for Space Technology. Naval Research Laboratory. http://code8100.nrl.navy.mil/. June 2007.

[216] Department of the Navy. *Spacecraft Engineering Department*. Naval Center for Space Technology. Naval Research Laboratory. http://code8200.nrl.navy.mil/. June 2007.

B. **CONCEPTS**

1. **Sea Power 21**

"SEA POWER 21" will guide our Navy as we defend our nation and defeat our enemies in the uncertain century before us. It will align our efforts, accelerate our progress, and realize the potential of our people.

SEA POWER 21 defines a Navy with three fundamental concepts: ***SEA SHIELD, SEA STRIKE, and the SEA BASE,*** enabled by ***FORCEnet***. Respectively, they enhance America's ability to project offensive power, defensive assurance, and operational independence around the globe. A supporting triad of initiatives will develop those core operational concepts: *Sea Warrior, SEA TRIAL,* and *Sea Enterprise*.

SEA SHIELD develops naval capabilities related to homeland defense, sea control, assured access, and projecting defense overland. By doing so, it reassures allies, strengthens deterrence, and protects the joint force.

SEA STRIKE is a broadened concept for naval power projection that leverages enhanced C4ISR, precision, stealth, and endurance to increase operational tempo, reach, and effectiveness.

The SEA BASE projects the sovereignty of the United States globally while providing Joint Force Commanders with vital command and control, fire support, and logistics from the sea, thereby minimizing vulnerable assets ashore.

Sea Warrior is the process of developing 21st century Sailors. It identifies the knowledge, skills, and abilities needed for mission accomplishment; applies a career-long training and education continuum; and employs a responsive, interactive career management system to ensure the right skills are in the right place at the right time.

SEA TRIAL is a continual process of concept and technology development through focused wargames, experiments, and exercises. It strengthens the Navy's culture of innovation and accelerates the delivery of enhanced capabilities to the Fleet.

Sea Enterprise captures efficiencies by employing lessons. From the business revolution to assess organizational alignment; target areas for improvement, and prioritize investments.

FORCEnet is an overarching effort to integrate warriors, sensors, networks, command and control, platforms, and weapons into a fully netted, combat force. FORCEnet will be the Navy's plan to make network-centric warfare an operational reality.[217]

Figure 13. Sea Power 21 Diagram[218]

2. **Coordinating Authority**

Coordinating authority may be exercised by commanders or individuals at any echelon at or below the level of combatant command. Coordinating authority is the authority delegated to a commander or individual for coordinating specific functions and activities involving forces of two or more Military Departments, two or more joint force components, or two or more forces of the same Service (e.g., joint rear area coordinator exercises coordinating authority for rear area operations among the component commanders). Coordinating authority may be granted and modified through a memorandum of agreement to provide unity of command and unity of effort for operations involving National Guard, Reserve

---

[217] Department of the Navy. *Sea Power 21*. Naval Warfare Development Command. http://www.nwdc.navy.mil/Concepts/Sea_Power_21/Sea_power_21.aspx. June 2007.

[218] Vern Clark, Admiral, U.S. Navy. *Sea Power 21. Projecting Decisive Joint Capabilities*. Naval Institute Proceedings. October 2002. http://www.navy.mil/navydata/cno/proceedings.html. June 2007.

Component (RC), and Active Component forces engaged in interagency activities. The commander or individual has the authority to require consultation between the agencies involved but does not have the authority to compel agreement. It is more applicable to planning and similar activities than to operations. Coordinating authority is not in any way tied to force assignment. Assignment of coordinating authority is based on the missions and capabilities of the commands or organizations involved.[219]

3. Space Authority

The space authority will coordinate space operations, integrate space capabilities, and have primary responsibility for in-theater joint space operations planning. The space authority will normally be supported by a JSST and will coordinate with the component SSTs and/or embedded space operators. It gathers space requirements throughout the joint force. While the space authority may facilitate non-traditional uses of space assets, joint force staffs should utilize the established processes when planning traditional Space Force Enhancement missions — intelligence, surveillance and reconnaissance; integrated tactical warning and attack assessment; environmental monitoring; communications; and navigation and timing. Following coordination, the space authority provides to the JFC a prioritized list of recommended space requirements based on the joint force objectives.[220]

4. Space Coordinating Authority (SCA)

The U.S. Air Force is currently the lead service with regards to space operations and planning. It is for this reason that the CFACC/COMAFFOR is granted the responsibility to serve as the space coordinating authority for a specific theater of operations. The JFC still maintains SCA at the JTF level.

5. Joint Warfighting Space

JWS brings space effects directly to the Joint Force Commander. Joint Warfighting Space will provide the following:

- Dedicated space forces: Expeditionary space and Near Space forces under control of the Joint Forces Commander

---

[219] United States. Joint Staff. *Joint Publication 0-2: Unified Action Armed Forces (UNAAF)*. Department of Defense, Washington D.C.: U.S. Government Printing Office. GL-6.

[220] United States. Joint Staff. *Joint Publication 3-14: Joint Doctrine for Space Operations*. Department of Defense. http://www.dtic.mil/doctrine/jel/new_pubs/jp3_14.pdf. Section III-3.

- Responsiveness: Usable capabilities in hours-to-days instead of days-to-weeks-to-months
- Integrated effects: Integrated with Global National Security Space and other theater systems[221]

6. Space Effects and Space Effects Packages

Space Effects Package example from the Fleet Space Handbook:[222]

SPACE ASSESSMENT:

- Status: SATCOM, GPS, ISR, METOC, Missile Warning

- Space Weather: Geomagnetic activity impact to HF Comm, charge particle impact to SATOPS

- GPS EMI: None reported in Theater

- SATCOM EMI: Service Advisory exists, resolution in progress by NIOSC Space, NCTAMS, and CSG N6

- Space Vulnerabilities: Space debris threat to Space assets, ASAT, GPS/SATCOM jammers, and SATVUL

SPACE OPERATIONS PLAN:

- Space Control
    - Surveillance
        - Monitor debris threat to Space assets and possible Space launches in vicinity of Strike Group operations.
    - Protection
        - Monitoring for potential GPS EMI to assure Position, Navigation, and Timing (PNT) for weapon systems.
        - Monitoring for SATCOM EMI to assure Over the Horizon (OTH) Command and Control (C2).
    - Prevention
        - Employ scheme of maneuver to prevent adversary from monitoring Strike Group operations from overhead.
    - Negation
        - If required, coordinate with DIRSPACEFOR to task.

---

[221] Department of the Air Force. *Operating Concept for Joint Warfighting Space (Draft)*. 13 January 2005. p. 15.

[222] Department of the Navy. Naval Network Warfare Command. *Fleet Space Handbook*. 2007. p. 16.

- Force Enhancement
    - Overhead Non-Imaging Infrared (ONIR) to detect infrared activity in vicinity of the Strike Group.
    - MASINT, task to support the ISR Plan
    - IMINT, task to support the ISR Plan

LIST OF REFERENCES

Alberts, David S., John J. Garstka, Frederick P. Stein. <u>Network Centric Warfare: Developing and Leveraging Information Superiority</u>. 2nd Edition. Library of Congress, Washington D.C. 1999.

Arthur, Daniel P. Lieutenant Commander, U.S. Navy and Dennis G. Wille, Major, U.S. Army. "A Proposed Architecture for Theater Coordination of Global Space Capabilities." Naval Postgraduate School Master's Thesis, Monterey, CA. 2006.

Barry, Tom. "Rumsfeld Space Commission." International Relations Center Right Web. 21 May 2004. <http://rightweb.irc-online.org/profile/2820>. (Last Accessed 5 June 2007.)

Black, Sam. "The Rhetoric of the Rumsfeld Space Commission." Center for Defense Information. 24 January 2007. <http://www.cdi.org/friendlyversion/printversion.cfm?documentID=3816>. (Last Accessed 12 June 2007.)

Boehm, Joshua and Craig Baker. "A History of United States National Security Space Management and Organization." Federation of American Scientists January 2001. <http://www.fas.org/spp/eprint/article03.html>. (Last Accessed 20 June 2007).

Clark, Vern. Admiral, U.S. Navy. "Sea Power 21. Projecting Decisive Joint Capabilities." Naval Institute Proceedings October 2002. <http://www.navy.mil/navydata/cno/proceedings.html>. (Last Accessed 27 June 2007).

Department of the Air Force. "14th Air Force Fact Sheet." <http://www.vandenburg.af.mil/library/factsheet/factsheet.asp?id=4684>. (Last Accessed 20 June 2007).

Department of the Air Force. "50th Space Wing Fact Sheet." Schriever Air Force Base. <http://www.schriever.af.mil/library/factsheets/factsheet.asp?id=3909>. (Last Accessed 20 June 2007).

Department of the Air Force. "50th Space Communications Squadron Fact Sheet." Schriever Air Force Base. <http://www.schriever.af.mil/library/factsheet/factsheet.asp?id=3917>. (Last Accessed 20 June 2007).

Department of the Air Force. <u>Air Force Doctrine Document 2, Operations and Organizations</u>. Washington D.C.: Government Printing Office, 27 June 2006.

Department of the Air Force. "Air Force Operational Tactics, Techniques, and Procedures 2-3.4, Joint Space Operations Center (Draft)." 2006.

Department of the Air Force. <u>Air Force Policy Directive 36-37 Personnel Space Professional Development</u>. 23 March 2006. <http://www.e-publishing.af.mil/pubfiles/af/36/afpd36-37/afpd36-37.pdf>. (Last Accessed 15 June 2007).

Department of the Air Force. "Air University Space Primer." 2003. <http://space.au.af.mil/primer/>. (Last Accessed 21 June 2007).

Department of the Air Force. "Emergence of the Strategic Air Command." 3 January 2006. Air Force Historical Studies Office. <https://www.airforcehistory.hq.af.mil/PopTopics/SAC.htm>. (Last Accessed 14 June 2007).

Department of the Air Force. "Operating Concept for Joint Warfighting Space (Draft)." 13 January 2005.

Department of the Air Force. "Operating Concept for Joint Warfighter Space (Draft)." 31 March 2005.

Department of the Navy. Assistant Secretary of the Navy, Research, Development & Acquisition. <http://acquisition.navy.mil/organizations>. (Last Accessed 29 May 2007).

Department of the Navy. June 2007. <http://forcenet.navy.mil/>. (Last Accessed 22 June 2007).

Department of the Navy. "Maritime Headquarters with Maritime Operations Center Concept of Operations (CONOPS), Final DRAFT Version." 15 May 2006.

Department of the Navy. "Naval Network Warfare Command Strategic Plan 2006-2010…a framework for decision-making. Executive Summary Version 2.0." <u>Naval Network Warfare Command</u>. 23 March 2007. <http://www.netwarcom.navy.mil/NETWARCOM%20Strategic%20Plan_Executive%20Version%202-0_1%2011.pdf>. (Last Accessed 27 June 2007).

Department of the Navy. Naval Network Warfare Command. *Fleet Space Handbook*. 2007.

Department of the Navy. Naval Network Warfare Command. "Navy Space Cadre Human Capital Strategy, Version 1.1." 27 December 2004.

126

Department of the Navy. Naval Satellite Operations Center. <http://www.nbvc.navy.mil/navsoc/detDelta.html>. (Last Accessed 25 May 2007).

Department of the Navy. "Navy Communications Satellite Programs. FactSheet: Ultra High Frequency Follow-On (UFO) Program." PMW-146. 1 March 1999. <http://www.globalsecurity.org/space/library/report/1999/uhf_follow-on_fact_sheet.pdf>. (Last Accessed 5 June 2007).

Department of the Navy. "Naval Center for Space Technology Mission Statement." Naval Research Laboratory. <http://www.ncst.nrl.navy.mil/homepage/mission.html>. (Last Accessed 25 June 2007).

Department of the Navy. "Naval Space Campaign Plan 2005-2007 'Space Capabilities For the Warfighter' 13 Nov 2005." Naval Network Warfare Command.

Department of the Navy. "Naval Research Laboratory Missions Statement." Naval Research Laboratory. <http://www.nrl.navy.mil/content.php?P=MISSION>. (Last Accessed 25 June 2007).

Department of the Navy. OPNAVINST 5400.43A Navy Space Policy Implementation. 12 February 2007. <https://doni.daps.dla.mil/Directives/Forms/AllItems.aspx?RootFolder=%2fDirectives%2f05000%20General%20Management%20Security%20and%20Safety%20Services%2f05%2d400%20Organization%20and%20Functional%20Support%20Services>. (Last Accessed 28 May 2007).

Department of the Navy. "PEO Space Systems Mission Statement." Space and Naval Warfare Systems Command. <http://enterprise.spawar.navy.mil/body.cfm?type=c&category=26&subcat=54>. (Last Accessed 31 May 2007).

Department of the Navy. "PMW-146 Missions Statement" Space and Naval Warfare Systems Command. <http://enterprise.spawar.navy.mil/pd14/pmw146/MISSION/mission_statement.htm>. (Last Accessed 31 May 2007).

Department of the Navy. "PMW-146 Organizational Chart." Space and Naval Warfare Systems Command. <http://enterprise.spawar.navy.mil/pd14/pmw146/index.htm>. (Last Accessed 17 June 2007).

Department of the Navy. "Sea Power 21." <u>Naval Warfare Development Command</u>. <http://www.nwdc.navy.mil/Concepts/Sea_Power_21/Sea_power_21.aspx>. (Last Accessed 13 June 2007).

Department of the Navy. <u>SECNAV Instruction 5400.39C: Department of Navy Space Policy</u>. 6 April 2004. <http://ftp.fas.org/irp/doddir/navy/secnavinst/5400_39c.pdf>. (Last Accessed 23 June 2007).

Department of the Navy. "Space and Naval Warfare Systems Command Center San Diego." <http://www.spawar.navy.mil/sandiego/>. (Last Accessed 22 June 2007).

Department of the Navy. "Spacecraft Engineering Department." Naval Center for Space Technology. <u>Naval research Laboratory</u>. <http://8200.nrl.navy.mil/>. (Last Accessed 25 June 2007).

Department of the Navy. "Space Systems Development Department." Naval Center for Space Technology. <u>Naval Research Laboratory</u>. <http://code8100.nrl.navy.mil/>. (Last Accessed 25 June 2007).

Department of the Navy. "The Carrier Strike Group." <http://www.navy.mil/navydata/ships/carriers/powerhouse/cvbg.asp>. (Last Accessed 6 June 2007).

Department of the Navy. "The SPAWAR Enterprise." <u>Space and Naval Warfare Systems Command</u>. <http://enterprise.spawar.navy.mil/UploadedFiles/SPAWAR%20Enterprise%20booklet%208.5x5.5.pdf>. (Last Accessed 1 June 2007).

Dinerman, Taylor. "The U.S. Navy: Lost in Space?" <u>The Space Review</u>. 24 October 2005. <http://www.thespacereview.com/article/480/1>. (Last Accessed 26 June 2007).

Dinerman, Taylor. "United States Space Force: sooner rather than later." <u>The Space Review</u>. 27 February 2006. <http://www.thespacereview.com/article/565/1>. (Last Accessed 27 June 2007).

Federici, Gary. "From the Sea to the Stars." <u>Naval Historical Center</u>. July 2003. <http://www.history.navy.mil/books/space/index.htm>. (Last Accessed 27 May 2007).

Galdorisi, George, Dr. Stephanie Hszieh and Terry McKearney. "SPAWAR Supports the Navy's Global Maritime Partnership" CHIPS. Apr-Jun 2007. <http://www.chips.navy.mil/archives/07_Jun/web_pages/Maritime_Partnership.html>. (Last Accessed 25 June 2007).

Gilmore, Gerry J. "Space 'Increasingly Important,' SPACECOM Chief Says" American Forces Press Service. 5 April 2001. <http://www.defenselink.mil/news/newsarticle.aspx?id=45030>. (Last Accessed 22 May 2007).

Hall, Kurt D. Lieutenant Colonel, U.S. Air Force. "Near Space: Should the Air Force Space Command Take Control of Its Shore?" Air University. September 2006. <http://aupress.maxwell.af.mil/Maxwell_Papers/Text/mp38.pdf>. (Last Accessed 21 June 2007).

Harter, Mark E. Lieutenant Colonel, U.S. Air Force. "10 Propositions Regarding Space Power, The Dawn of a Space Force." Air and Space Journal. 1 June 2006. <http://www.airpower.maxwell.af.mil/airchronicles/apj/apj06/sum06/harter.html> (Last Accessed 27 June 2007).

Hicks, Joel, Commander, US Navy. Excerpts from e-mail to the Authors, titled: "Re:Questions regarding NAVSOC." 15 June 2007.

Insch, Paul M. Captain, U.S. Navy. "NAVSOC Command Brief." Naval Satellite Operations Center. PowerPoint Brief. June 2006.

Jenner, Lynn. "Dr. Robert H. Goddard: American Rocket Pioneer." NASA. December 2004. <http://www.nasa.gov/centers/goddard/about/dr_goddard.html>. (Last Accessed 29 May 2007).

Johnson, Kevin. Commander, U.S. Navy. "Re: NSSI Shortfalls." E-mail among NETWARCOM N36, N1, CSG-8 N39, NSC Advisor. 11 January 2007.

Lambeth, Benjamin S. Mastering the Ultimate High Ground: Next Steps in the Military Uses of Space. RAND Corporation. 2003. <http://www.rand.org/pubs/monograph_reports/MR1649/>. (Last Accessed 7 June 2007).

Leszczynski, Zigmond, Commander, U.S. Navy. "EISENHOWER Strike Group (IKESG) End-of-Deployment, Space Segment." 25 May 2007.

Leszczynski, Zigmond, Commander, U.S. Navy. "Space Training, Education and Community Support." PowerPoint Brief, March 2005.

Mitchell, Eddie. Apogee, Perigee, and Recovery: Chronology of Army Exploitation of Space. Santa Monica, CA: Rand, 1991.

Mullen, Michael. Admiral, U.S. Navy. "CNO Guidance for 2006." Department of the Navy. <http://www.navy.mil/features/2006CNOG.pdf>. (Last Accessed 11 June 2007).

National Research Council, Naval Studies Board. The Navy's Needs in Space For Providing Future Capabilities. Washington, D.C: January 2005 <http://www.nap.edu/books/0309096774/html>. (Last Accessed 21 June 2007).

Navy Knowledge Online. March 2007. Space Succession Plan: NSC billets as of March 2007. <https://www.nko.navy.mil>. (Last Accessed 15 June 2007).

Navy League of the United States. "Spinning the Web. An interview with Vice Adm. Richard W. Mayo, Commander, Naval Network Warfare Command." Sea Power. ProQuest Information and Learning Company. April 2003. <http://findarticles.com/p/articles/mi_qa3738/is_200304/ai_n9225120/pg_3>. (Last Accessed 4 June 2007).

Niedermaier, Julie, Commander, U.S. Navy. "Navy Space Cadre Update (SSFA Space Indoctrination)." PowerPoint Brief. March 2007.

Office of the Assistant Secretary of Defense (Public Affairs). "Secretary Rumsfeld Announces Major National Security Space Management and Organizational Initiative." 201-01. 8 May 2001. DefenseLink. <http://www.defenselink.mil/releases/release.aspx?releaseid=2908>. (Last Accessed 13 June 2007).

Peters, F.W. and Michael E. Ryan. "The Aerospace Force: Defending America in the 21st Century...a White Paper on Aerospace Integration." 23 August 2003. U.S. Air Force. <http://stinet.dtic.mil/cgibin/GetTRDoc?AD=ADA381077&Location=U2&doc= GetTRDoc.pdf>. (Last Accessed 28 May 2007).

See, Victor. Rear Admiral, U.S. Navy. "Interview with Rear Adm. Victor See Jr., Director, Communications Systems Acquisition and Operations Directorate, NRO; Commander, SPAWAR Space Field Activity; PEO Space Systems." CHIPS. March 2006. <http://www.chips.navy.mil/archives/06_Jan/web_pages/RADM_SEE.htm>. (Last Accessed 8 June 2007).

Stares, Paul B. The Militarization of Space, U.S. Policy 1945-1948. Ithaca, N.Y.: Cornell University Press, 1985.

Time Magazine. "Aerospace Force?" 17 March 1961. <http://www.time.com/time/magazine/article/0,9171,894428,00.html>. (Last Accessed 17 June 2007).

United States. Department of Defense. Joint Staff. <u>Chairman of the joint Chiefs of Staff Instruction 6250.01B "Satellite Communications</u>. 28 May 2004.

United States. Department of Defense. <u>Department of Defense Directive 5160.32: Development of Space Systems</u>. March 1961. <http://www.dtic.mil/whs/directives/index.html>. (Last Accessed 13 June 2007)

United States. Department of Defense. <u>Department of Defense Directive 5101.2: DoD Executive Agent For Space</u>. 22 July 2003. <http://www.dtic.mil/whs/directives/corres/html/510102.htm>. (Last Accessed 26 June 2007).

United States. Department of Defense. Joint Staff. <u>Joint Publication 0-2: Unified Action, Armed Forces</u>. Washington D.C.: U.S. Government Printing Office, 10 July 2001.

United States. Department of Defense, Joint Staff. <u>Joint Publication 3-14: Joint Doctrine for Space Operations</u>. Washington, D.C: U.S. Government Printing Office, 9 August 2002. <http://www.dtic.mil/doctrine/jel/new_pubs/jp3_14.pdf>. (Last Accessed 28 June 2007).

United States. Department of Defense. <u>Report of the Commission to Assess United States National Security Space Management and Organization</u>. 12 January 2001. <http://www.dod.mil/pubs/space20010111.html>. (Last Accessed 28 June 2007).

United States. Department of Defense. "Space Program Executive Overview for FY1998-2003." March 1997. <http://www.fas.org/spp/military/program/sp97>. (Last Accessed 14 June 2007).

United States. Government Accountability Office. <u>Report to Congressional Committees: DEFENSE SPACE ACTIVITIES: Additional Actions Needed to Implement Human Capital Strategy and Develop Space Personnel</u>. August 2004. <http://www.gao.gov/new.items/d04697.pdf>. (Last Accessed 19 June 2007).

United States. Government Accountability Office. <u>Report to Congressional Committees, DEFENSE SPACE ACTIVITIES: Management Guidance and Performance Measures needed to Develop Personnel</u>. September 2005. <http://www.gao.gov/cgi-bin/getrpt?GAO-05-833>. (Last Accessed 20 June 2007).

United States. House Armed Services Committee. "SPACE CADRE/SPACE PROFESSIONALS Hearing Before the Strategic Forces Subcommittee of the Committee on Armed Services House of Representatives." H.A.S.C. No. 108–40. 22 July 2004. <http://commdocs.house.gov/committees/security/has204290.000/has204290_0f.htm>. (Last Accessed 20 June 2007).

United States. House Armed Services Committee. "Statement of Brigadier General Thomas A. Benes, Director, Strategy and Plans Division. Plans, Policies, and Operation Department. Headquarters, United States Marine Corps." Space Budget Activities. 9 March 2005. <http://www.globalsecurity.org/space/library/congress/2005_h/050309-benes.pdf>. (Last Accessed 5 July 2007).

United States. "National Reconnaissance Office Vision and Mission Statement." National Reconnaissance Office. <http://www.nro.gov>. (Last Accessed 29 May 2007).

United States. Senate Armed Services Committee. "Interview of Vice Admiral Joseph A. Sestak, U.S. Navy, Deputy Chief of Naval Operations (Warfare Requirements and Programs) before the Strategic Forces Subcommittee of the Senate Armed Services Committee." FY2006 Defense Authorization Budget Request for Space Activities. 16 March 2005. <http://www.navy.mil/navydata/testimony/technology/sestak050316.txt>. (Last Accessed 6 June 2007).

United States. United States National Space Policy. 31 August 2006. <http://www.ostp.gov/html/US%20National%20Space%20Policy.pdf>. (Last Accessed 20 May 2007).

Voltz, Toby. Lieutenant Colonel. U.S. Air Force. "Joint Warfighting Concept of Operations." PowerPoint Brief. 5 December 2005.

Wagner, Gary R. "Navy Transfers Space Surveillance Mission to Air Force." Naval Network and Space Operations Command Public Affairs, Navy Newstand. 20 October 2004. <http://www.navy.mil/search/display.asp?story_id=15597>. (Last Accessed 12 June 2007).

Wiesner Committee."Report to the President-Elect of the Ad Hoc Committee on Space." 10 January 1961. NASA History Office. <http://www.hq.nasa.gov/office/pao/History/report61.html>. (Last Accessed 5 June 2007).

Wilbur, Ted. "Navy Space." Naval Aviation News. November 1970.

INITIAL DISTRIBUTION LIST

1. Defense Technical Information Center
   Ft. Belvoir, VA

2. Dudley Knox Library
   Naval Postgraduate School
   Monterey, CA

3. Commander Michelle Hillmeyer, USN
   NETWARCOM
   Little Creek, VA

4. Captain (sel) Julie Neidermaier
   OPNAV N1/NETWARCOM
   Washington D.C.

5. Captain Diana Cangelosi, USN
   Naval Satellite Operations Center (NAVSOC)
   Point Mugu, CA

6. RDML Victor C. See, Jr., USN
   PEO Space Systems
   Chantilly, VA

7. Mr. Bob Tarleton
   PMW-146
   San Diego, CA

8. ADM Robert Willard, USN
   Commander, U.S. Pacific Fleet
   Pearl Harbor, HI

9. VADM H. Denby Starling II, USN
   Commander, NETWARCOM
   Little Creek, VA